*Essays by member
Archbishops' Commission on*

Thinking about tl

*With a Preface by Ian T. Ramsey,
Bishop of Durham*

SCM PRESS LTD

334 01651 7
First published 1972
by SCM Press Ltd
56 Bloomsbury Street, London
© SCM Press Ltd 1972
Printed in Great Britain by
Northumberland Press Limited
Gateshead

Contents

Preface   iv
The Right Reverend Ian T. Ramsey, Bishop of Durham

1 The Philosophical Background to Eucharistic Theology   1
  J. R. Lucas, Fellow of Merton College, Oxford

2 Matter in the Theological and Scientific Perspectives – A Sacramental View   14
  The Reverend Dr A. R. Peacocke, Fellow of St Peter's College, Oxford

3 The 'Institution' Narratives and the Christian Eucharist   38
  The Reverend John Austin Baker, Chaplain and Lecturer in Divinity, Corpus Christi College, Oxford

4 The Eucharist and Symbolism in the New Testament   59
  The Reverend C. F. Evans, Professor of New Testament Studies, University of London King's College

5 Symbols and the Eucharist   68
  The Right Reverend Hugh Montefiore, Bishop of Kingston-upon-Thames

6 Sacrifice and the Eucharist   81
  The Reverend J. L. Houlden, Principal of Cuddesdon College, Oxford

7 The Eucharistic Presence   99
  The Reverend Dr H. E. W. Turner, Canon of Durham and van Mildert Professor of Theology in the University of Durham

8 Eucharistic Theology – The Value of Diversity   115
  The Reverend M. F. Wiles, Canon of Christ Church and Regius Professor of Divinity in the University of Oxford

Preface

Ian T. Ramsey
Bishop of Durham

The essays contained in this volume arose from a request made to the Archbishops' Commission on Christian Doctrine when the Church of England Liturgical Commission was preparing the Series III order of the eucharist. We were asked for comments on certain issues which had arisen in liturgical discussion, and to help set these issues against a wider background of eucharistic theology, members of the Doctrine Commission contributed specific papers on relevant themes. These papers were subsequently revised in the light of discussion, and are now published as a contribution to further study of the eucharist. They have the status of Occasional Papers which it has been the custom of the Doctrine Commission, with the consent of the Archbishops, to publish in order to help forward profitable debate on important doctrinal issues, and while they have benefited from general discussion, each paper carries the authority only of its author.

All the essays represent an endeavour to think afresh and in broader contexts about the eucharist, and in doing so to display an eirenic rather than a sectarian spirit.

Mr Lucas approaches the topic by way of philosophical enquiry, which asks questions about the logic of action, the character of corporate activity and the fundamental significance of eating and drinking, of giving and being given in return. It is because the eucharist is primarily an action that we cannot talk of it 'apart from its intention, meaning or significance' (p. 11). This is why, as he says, 'many different understandings of the eucharist are possible, and perhaps valid, and why many different eucharistic practices have grown up'. While 'not all understandings of the eucharist are equally valid and some are to be rejected as altogether inadequate', we ought nevertheless to be 'cautious in denying what we may regard as the erroneous opinions of others' (p. 12).

Dr Peacocke, approaching the eucharist as a scientist, believes 'that there can be a mutual enrichment of Christian incarnational and sacramental insights by the scientific perspective and *vice versa*' (p. 32). Dr Peacocke sees the eucharist as a microcosm of God's creativity in the world culminating in Christ, and he would, I believe, think of the eucharistic pattern of speech-acts as a distinctive organization, comparable with the new organizations of matter which form the creative pattern of evolution, but more particularly bearing the impress of the unique activity of God in Christ.

By a critical appraisal of the 'institution' narratives, which both challenges many conventional assumptions, and clarifies some traditional problems, Mr Baker gives us a New Testament prolegomena to present-day liturgical concerns. He suggests that it is 'because the institution narratives were later regarded as liturgical directives that the church's life and witness have been disfigured by the misery of eucharistic dissension' (pp. 55f.). The result of the new approach which Mr Baker would counsel is that New Testament scholarship legitimizes certain new freedoms whether in the content and construction of our eucharistic prayers or in the matter of theological speculation. It broadens our perspective to see that 'a eucharist (must) have post-resurrection existence as its axis' (p. 56).

Many speak of the eucharist as a 'symbolic meal', and Professor Christopher Evans and Bishop Hugh Montefiore are both concerned with broader questions of symbolism. The earlier essay is concerned with the intricate, not to say baffling, way in which biblical symbols operate; the later essay, broadening 'eucharistic theology' into 'worship thinking', attempts to identify some of the symbols and images of the eucharist, and the feeling and the sentiments with which these images and symbols are generally associated.

The next two essays concern themselves with themes that have for long been traditional and divisive in eucharistic theology: sacrifice and presence. Mr Houlden's essay, while recognizing that sacrificial language has always had a very prominent place in eucharistic thinking and certainly preserves some important truths about the eucharist, shows that even here the variegation has been immense and often problematical.

Professor Turner offers us an interpretation of our Lord's presence in the eucharist in personal terms, and explores the possibility of such an interpretation doing justice to traditional themes. His exploration leads us in a direction which is neither that of the *nuda signa* of Zwingli nor of a doctrine of transubstantiation. He rightly remarks that some careful qualifications of the personalist interpretation will be necessary if, for instance, we would relate the eucharistic presence to the whole of eucharistic action, but this is simply to underline the multiple character of eucharistic theology.

Professor Wiles glances back, in effect, over all the essays and develops independently this theme which has recurred throughout the book—the need to acknowledge a wide diversity in eucharistic understanding and practice. Such a variety is a valuable and not a regrettable feature of eucharistic theology, something that may illuminate what otherwise may seem not only very puzzling but unanswerable questions, e.g. about what is or is not 'a eucharist', questions which have generated talk which, in its turn, has only served to sharpen division among Christians.

To acknowledge theological diversity is not to sell out to theological relativism. It is rather an admission that we shall always need many theological strands to understand 'the unsearchable riches of Christ' and it certainly places on us the task of constant analysis and cross-referencing. This is the kind of activity that must characterize not only eucharistic theology but all theology as its central task. Indeed, in so far as these essays illustrate a way of thinking about the eucharist that implies a multiple theology, they are not only valuable in themselves, but provide significant evidence of the new era in theology. It would be hard to exaggerate the change of attitude which a multiple theology nurtures, as compared with a theology supposed to be a subject apart, monolithic, and determinative of conclusions in all other subjects, be they science or history. That change is but one measure of the cultural revolution into which we are moving.

I

The Philosophical Background to Eucharistic Theology

J. R. Lucas

If a stranger were to attend a celebration of the eucharist he would say that the people involved were *doing* something. They were saying things, sometimes to one another, sometimes together. Something was being eaten and something drunk. In some rites he might say further that something was being given, and something given back. And, if he were sensitive to atmosphere, he might add that the proceedings meant something very significant to all concerned.

These bare descriptions – doing, doing together, saying, eating, drinking, giving, being given back, meaning – are the strands which our Lord, and at his bidding the church, have woven together in instituting the eucharist. We cannot expound it as being merely a performance, a corporate activity, a seminar, a common meal, an offertory, a reception, or a symbolic rite, for it is more than all these. Nevertheless it is these. These were features of the Last Supper, as they had been of the Passover in ancient Israel, which enabled it to be what our Lord intended it to be, and it is these features that have enabled the Lord's Supper, the eucharist, the mass, the holy communion, and the early service to be the focus of the church's corporate life on earth and the main way whereby the individual Christian can enter into a relationship with God. They underly, although they do not exhaust, all our thinking about the eucharist.

In celebrating the eucharist we do something. The logic of action is very different from the logic of things. Actions are not exclusive in the way that things are. We say that Solomon built the Temple, but do not thereby deny that many artificers and craftsmen built it too. Or to take a more modern example, when we say that Baden-Powell created the Boy Scout movement, we do not in the least belittle the dedicated work of many others who equally well could be said to have brought it into being. And so too the action of twentieth-century men in celebrating the eucharist neither excludes, nor is excluded by, its being also the action of our Lord Jesus Christ who on the night that he was betrayed said, 'Do this ...'.

Not only can different people do the same actions, but any action can be described in many different ways. I turn my finger, I twiddle the dial, I ring up my agent, I hatch a plot, I let the side down, I forward my own ambitions – all these may be apt descriptions of the same bodily behaviour. Which descriptions are right is often a matter of great controversy and cannot be settled by reference to overt behaviour alone. Actions are instinct with reasons. *What* we do depends on *why* we are doing it. And therefore how we describe an action will depend in part on what reasons we ascribe to the agent. There are often various different reasons for which we undertake some particular action, and so different descriptions may be given, all equally correct. It may be correct to describe the eucharist as a commemoration of Christ's death: but it does not follow that it is not also a fellowship meal at which he himself is present.

The same bodily behaviour can be correctly described as different actions. It is also part of the logic of action that different patterns of bodily behaviour can be accounted the same action. I can buy a car by going into a shop, handing over money, and driving away; or by writing a letter; or by nodding at an auction. My bodily movements are far from being the same, but are in each case appropriate in their context to bring about the result I desire; and if the situation had been different, my movements would have been different, too – if the auctioneer had not been looking straight at me, I would have waved my arm or shouted something. Actions are what cyberneticians call homeostatic processes – the actual bodily behaviour depends on the situation in such a way as to bring about the desired state of affairs in spite of variation of the circumstances. And therefore when we describe a particular pattern of bodily behaviour as an action, we not only are describing what actually happened but are saying that *if* the conditions *had been* slightly different, an appropriately different pattern of bodily behaviour *would have been* manifested. That is to say, as soon as we talk of actions we are talking not only in the indicative mood, of what actually was or will be seen, but in the subjunctive mood too. Actions have a logical depth that things and events lack, and concern not only what appears on the surface

The Philosophical Background to Eucharistic Theology 3

and what can be recorded by the camera, but what might have been done or would have been done, had things been different.

The paradigm actions are those of an individual – what I do, what you do or what he does. But we also talk in the plural, of what we do and what they do, and it is a profound fact of the human condition that men are vitally concerned with the first person plural as much as with the first person singular. I identify. It matters to me what my children, my colleagues, my compatriots, do. I have views about what *we* ought to do, am proud of our achievements when we have done well, and am ashamed of our failures and mistakes and everything that we have done badly. I would not be myself if I were not, besides being an individual, also a member of many different communities and associations, whose well-being is part and parcel of my own individual well-being. *How* this is so, is a matter of philosophical dispute: but *that* it is so can scarcely be denied. And it is one of the tenets of Christianity that we are all members one of another, and that in the eucharist we join in an activity which is essentially corporate.

A corporate activity is not simply a number of individuals acting individually. If I go into a snack-bar and eat a meal, and you go into a snack-bar and eat a meal, it does not follow that we have had a meal together. It is not enough that we each do the same thing: what is essential is that each does whatever he does in the light, and on account, of the other's doings. It may be that we are all doing the same thing – as when we sing in unison together: or it may be that we are doing different things – as when we sing in harmony, or play football, or conduct research: but in either case I take the actions of others as my cue, and make my own contribution harmonize with what other people are doing. Their actions are the context in which I act, and we share the same purpose, even if our individual contributions to its realization need to be different. The essential condition is not that we all do the same individual actions, but that we all share the same concern, and are aware of one another acting from that concern. Since our knowledge of other people is never complete, we can achieve our corporate activity only by assuming certain rôles. A team can be effective only if everyone can rely on one man being near the goal and another acting as centre-forward. In small groups the amount of rôle-playing may be fairly small, but in large groups it becomes paramount. Only the Queen can dissolve Parliament, only a jury can find a man guilty of murder, only a judge impose a penalty, only a university award a degree. From this flows a certain impersonality. Britain would still have been Britain and would still have won the war if I had never been born. The University of Oxford would have continued to exist and would have given substantially the same degrees if I had never been one of its examiners. It is part of the meaning of the word 'community' that no one of us is logically indispensable: societies are in this sense, as the French call them, *'sociétés anonymes'*. The original meaning of the word 'parson' was that of 'rôle-player'; and the church has often found it necessary to distinguish between his representative and his individual character. We can join in the eucharistic liturgy only because it is a ritual which assigns to us particular responses at particular times: and in joining in it, we act not only as individuals but as members of Christ's body dispersed over the face of the earth and down the ages.

The most sophisticated ritual we have is language. The celebration of the Lord's Supper has always been conjoined with the communication of the Good News, and would in itself be entirely unintelligible apart from the events recounted in the canon, the intuitions expressed, and the petitions made. Nevertheless, much of the ritual is more primitive, and perhaps more fundamental, than that of language, and it is helpful to leave consideration of the language used until later, and to view the eucharist first as a corporate meal. For this it was, and is. For reasons given by St Paul, it early became a stylized meal in which the eating and drinking were attenuated to the very minimum, and in some parts of Christendom the cup was denied the laity. But always the bread has been broken and shared and eaten. And this in itself means a lot.

The sharing of a meal is the most fundamental sort of sharing for human beings because the need for food and drink is the one need we all share and are continually being made aware of. Many other values may be cherished by many men in common – a love of England, or of mediaeval architecture, or of mathematical logic: but not everyone loves England or mediaeval architecture or mathematical logic, and any corporate activity centred on these as their focus of common concern would necessarily be selective and exclusive. But we all know that we need food and drink and therefore all value food and drink, and regard them as good. To offer a man a morsel or to give him a drink is a gesture that cannot but be taken as a token of good will; and to join in eating and drinking is to engage in a common activity which each, however individualistic his standpoint, must regard as desirable and good. And although it is possible

The Philosophical Background to Eucharistic Theology 5

to satisfy one's bodily hunger in isolation, it is in another sense very unsatisfactory to so do, and the solitary eater, like the solitary drinker, is an object of pity and compassion. Wherever possible we eat and drink in company, and only in company is either really satisfying.

Ancient Israel, like the modern West, placed great emphasis on the nuclear family, father and mother and the young children like olive branches round the table. The Passover had something of the same significance that Christmas dinner has. The Last Supper, however, was eaten by a group of friends, and the Christian eucharist generally has had the air more of a celebration of a peer-group than of a family. It is a more easily inclusive form of organization – a stranger invited to a Christmas dinner still feels awkward and something of an interloper, whereas there is no blood barrier to feeling at home in a college hall or at a regimental dinner. Since the gospel was universal, and any man might become a son of God by adoption of the Spirit, it was important not to emphasize too much the natural ties of blood relationships. Again, families are small, whereas the churches soon waxed large; large groups are much less closely knit than small ones; and in large congregations, the holy communion is not so much a corporate activity as an individual one – and an individual one in which most individuals play a relatively passive part. Only if every householder were a priest could the eucharist be entirely a family affair. And again, in the ancient world, as now, there were many people who had no family life but were not to be excluded from communion with God – slaves crept out in the early morning to celebrate the eucharist while their masters were still asleep. The eucharist was more a reunion dinner than a family one in the strict sense. It took up a long tradition in the Greek world. The Spartans had always eaten together, and occasional fellowship meals were common elsewhere. Epicurus left money in his will for memorial meals, much as many colleges now have feasts in commemoration of founders and benefactors. Even when we are drawn together by a shared sorrow, we still find it appropriate to express our fellow feeling by also eating and drinking together. The Last Supper was the funeral bakemeats for our Lord's death, and the weekly eucharist parallels in part the 'year's mind', when we remember the departed, and in our sadness also rejoice. On such occasions it is natural and correct to ascribe the activity of those present to the influence of the deceased, and even to say that he brought about the things that they do. Keble College owes its existence to John

Keble, and would not have existed but for him, and has, to some extent, been the embodiment of his spirit. We may also go further and say, more metaphorically, that the dead man still lives in the memory and activity of his friends, or the teacher in the minds of his pupils, or the composer in his symphonies, or the founder in his foundation. This is not to claim immortality. Rather, it is to view human beings as, primarily, agents, and therefore to say that they are what they do, and, hence also, what they achieve through the agency of other men's actions. The spirit of Epicurus lives in the intellectual friendships and philosophical discussions of his disciples, especially when they are all gathered together in his name, and doing the things he wanted them to do and had in his own time done himself. And so too the Christians, when they express their corporate solidarity by eating and drinking together, may also remember their master, and feel that he still lives in their common life.

But it is a very thin life. Jeremy Bentham, like Epicurus, hoped that the young men of University College, London, would continue to be convivial after his death and spare a kindly thought for him, but added the further provision that his corpse, which was to be embalmed and kept in University College, should attend these parties, so that he might be present in the flesh. It is a macabre idea, but expresses the sense of inadequacy of being there merely in spirit. If the Lord's Supper were merely a fellowship meal in which Christians looked back to the Passion and remembered Jesus Christ, it would be similarly inadequate: but the Lord's Supper is also the Lord's because, in the light of the resurrection, he is present, and we are supping with him, as we look as much forward to the future as back to the past. It is the Lord Mayor's banquet, with the Lord Mayor present, and everyone celebrating his accession to power.

The future is very different from the past. We can keep on commemorating the same event, but we cannot keep on inaugurating the same era. I can only once come of age, a wedding can only once be celebrated, and the Second Coming, when it comes, will come only once. It follows that the celebration of the eucharist which we, in accordance with our Lord's command, repeat day by day or week by week, cannot be exactly the inaugural banquet of Christ's accession. We can, in part, see in the eucharist a foretaste of a greater banquet yet to come: we can liken it to the Queen's Accession service, a thanksgiving for Christ's triumph, which is still, and will continue to be, effective in our lives; but in order to get the full

The Philosophical Background to Eucharistic Theology

force of the immediate forward-looking aspect of the eucharist we have to make a slightly sophisticated change of reference. Rather than think of it as the Lord Mayor's banquet, given by a particular Lord Mayor, we need to compare it with a more generalized celebration of inauguration. In our culture we should compare it with New Year parties. These can be repeated, and yet are indisputably oriented towards the future. As we see the New Year in, we do not suppose that 1972 will be an entirely new sort of existence in contrast to 1971: our celebration is not tied to the particularity of the year, but to the generality of the newness. And in the eucharist we celebrate the fact that we are granted newness of life, not merely as a matter of secular fact, but in the life of the Spirit. Thanks to Christ's death and resurrection, we can go forward in confidence and look to the future in hope. A new possibility having been opened for us by Christ, we are realizing it for ourselves every time we share the Lord's Supper with the brethren, and *ta men opisō epilanthanomenoi tois de emprosthen epekteinometha* (cf. Phil. 3.13b), forgetting what is behind, reach out to that which lies ahead. The eucharist is not merely a memorial of things long past, but is the expression of a doctrine of *epektasis*, and an effective implementation of it in our lives, a weekly New Day's party to celebrate the fact that by virtue of the resurrection we shall always be finding new things to do, new things worth doing, new ways of making each his own contribution, new treasures still of countless price, new thoughts of God, new hopes of heaven.

Although the Last Supper was a supper, and some of the earliest celebrations of the eucharist may have been suppers too, there was from New Testament times onwards a tendency to whittle down the meal to a purely symbolic form. Some of the reasons were practical. In addition to those of decorum given by St Paul, a real meal is relatively costly, and the early church did not have the odd two hundred denarii available to ensure that all should be filled. Banquets, although real, tend to be expensive and exclusive. If the poor are to be able to be filled with the good things from the Lord's table, only nominal amounts of bread and wine can be handed out, which must act as tokens of what is being given us. But this attenuation of the supper to the eucharist both requires and automatically heightens a symbolic interpretation. Just because we are not getting very much to eat and drink, we are impelled to understand what we are doing as not being merely eating and drinking. One, not very satisfactory, explanation is the vitamin-pill model of Ignatius. It makes sense to describe the elements as *pharmakon athanasiās*, 'immortality pill', if taken in very small quantities, whereas it would be difficult to make out that an English Christmas dinner was 'medicine'. We all feel the force of the homeopathic argument that the tablets and the mixture are shown to be potent by reason of the fact that they have to be taken in very, very small doses. And once the eucharist ceases to be a real meal, it is dangerously easy to apply a similar argument there.

There is a tension between different requirements. Unless the Lord's Supper is celebrated by our really eating food and really imbibing drink, we lose the basic principle that it is a good thing for every one who joins in: but unless we are prepared to sit loose to the satisfaction of our bodily hunger and thirst, we may lose sight of the principle that it is something more than merely physical satisfaction. Although we can emphasize some symbolic effect by acting counter to natural expectations, there is a perpetual danger that in so doing we may destroy the basis on which the whole symbolism rests. For this reason the current antithesis between the *agape* and the eucharist is unfortunate. They are not so much opposed as having had different aspects emphasized. In a wedding reception a man with a weak digestion might eat only a morsel of wedding cake and drink only a sip of champagne for the toast; and if the bride's father was very poor, or there was great need for secrecy or speed, everyone would be content to do only this. Normally, however, we like to set the cutting of the cake and the drinking of the toast in a wider context of jollification, and feel that there are better ways of expressing the overtones of the event than by having only very exiguous supplies of eats and drinks. We criticize the man who indulges in them too freely, as St Paul did, as also the women who continue to chatter during the bridegroom's speech. The wedding reception is not merely a free meal. It is meant to mean something, and this is expressed by certain things being said and done at a certain time, and everyone should then attend and join in, and if need be, everything else could be stripped away, and we should be content with a bare cutting and distribution of cake and drinking of the toast. But this is the exceptional case, and draws its significance from the general context which most wedding receptions provide. Similarly in the Lord's Supper, the eating and drinking may be attenuated to a purely symbolic eating and drinking, without thereby losing its significance, but it does not have to be thus attenuated in order to secure its significance. A eucharist does not have to be an *agape*,

The Philosophical Background to Eucharistic Theology

but an *agape* does not have to be not a eucharist. There may be occasions when an *agape* is specially designed not to be a eucharist – e.g. to avoid difficulties about intercommunion – just as there might be a gathering after a wedding intended not to be a wedding reception – e.g. if one of the parties were a *divorcé* – and in either case this would be signalled by leaving out the traditional actions – no wedding-cake, no wine, no speeches, only tea and biscuits. But so great is the power of the underlying symbolism of eating and drinking in common that it is a precarious distinction that is being drawn, and very soon the tea-fight takes on the characteristics of a reception, and the *agape* becomes a eucharist.

The eucharist is not only a matter of eating and drinking, but of giving and of being given in return. We give bread and wine to God – particularly in the congregational liturgies of England and America – and in our turn we are given a morsel of bread to eat and a sip of wine to drink. It is easy to view the giving in each direction as symbolic: the people of God offer up the fruits of their labours, their work, and God gives us not merely the means of physical sustenance, but himself, his Spirit, to enliven and fortify us as we go forth into the world. This interpretation is natural and meaningful in the twentieth century, and valid so far as it goes. But Christ need not have died on the cross to institute a service of communal dedication and re-invigoration. Even in the fourth century it was felt to be inadequate. Who are we to presume to offer God gifts? To give and be given in return either suggests a mechanical or commercial transaction or else presumes a personal relationship already established which it is the point of the communion in part to secure for us. It is only because we have first been invited to share with Christ in God's banquet that we are on a footing to offer any contribution of our own. Giving, if it does not degenerate into trading, is in danger of becoming Pelagianism. The only really relevant self-giving in the eucharist is that of Christ. But Christ gave himself for us and our salvation in a number of different ways: in coming down from heaven and becoming a man; in his life of ministry on earth; in founding a church; in dying on the cross; in his continual fellowship with men after the resurrection until the ascension; in sending the Holy Spirit; in his continuing fellowship with men in the Holy Spirit from Pentecost until now; and in his coming again at the Last Day to judge both the quick and the dead. And in as much as Christ had different reasons for doing any one of these, still further differences of description may be apt. The same difficulties about time and tense that occurred in the characterization of the fellowship meal will beset any description of the eucharist as the self-giving of Christ. In the most obvious sense – in dying on the cross – Christ gave himself in the aorist tense, once, only once, and once for all. We may legitimately extend this to the perfect tense, in as much as the past event still has present effects, but cannot use the present tense to suggest that this self-giving could either be repeated or regarded as still occurring. In other, admittedly less obvious or less central, senses of self-giving, Christ can be said still to give or be giving himself, and the eucharist can be intelligibly described in such terms. But there is still the difficulty, not present in the characterization of most actions, that self-giving is a reflexive concept, and that therefore, although we may imitate Christ's self-giving by offering up our own work and lives, we cannot associate ourselves with Christ's self-giving, as we can in carrying out his will in other ways. The eucharist, regarded as the fulfilment of our Lord's command, can be both his action and ours: but we cannot offer up Christ to the Father as an act of self-giving in the primary sense. Only he could do that.

There are still senses in which we can describe the eucharist in terms of self-giving. Quite apart from specifically Christian doctrines, any personal relationship involves each party giving himself in some degree to the other: and therefore it is built into any rite of holy communion that in it God gives himself to those who come to meet him. More specifically, Christians believe that they can be at one with God, only because Christ gave himself for us on the cross. For these reasons, various understandings of the eucharist, although less natural than that in terms of a shared meal, are nonetheless valid. Their validity depends not on natural congruity, but on the fact that our Lord intended it, both because the Last Supper was (if we accept the synoptic chronology) a celebration of the Passover, and because it took place on the eve, and under the shadow, of the crucifixion, and, further, because of his teaching and example in his earthly ministry. The ways in which the modern eucharist can properly be understood in terms of self-giving should be based, not on *a priori* argument, but on what we believe our Lord intended. It is a matter not of philosophy, but of New Testament scholarship.

The eucharist is significant. It is meant to mean something. In it we approach God as a person, not only in word – by addressing prayers to him and listening to the Bible – but in all our actions and attitudes, which are intended to show forth our adoration for him

The Philosophical Background to Eucharistic Theology

and his love for us. But our words are inadequate and our actions may be misunderstood. Although Christians believe that God is personal, and that through Christ we can enter into some sort of personal relationship with him, we find it very difficult to give an account of this personal relationship – indeed, the word 'personal' is itself open to criticism – and often we fall back on the terminology of legal or logical or causal relationships. Such metaphors are natural, and to many people helpful: but they can mislead, and when we come to talk about the eucharist we often are tempted to press the wrong questions or to describe it in terms inappropriate to a living God who loves us and wants us to know him even as we are known. Equally with our actions, when we come to explain their significance we often describe them as symbolic, and obscurely feel that if they are symbolic, there must be a difference between what they are and what they mean. Symbols, we feel, are mere representations of something else for which they stand, in the same way as a picture symbolizes a scene it resembles while being essentially different from it. But this is a mistake. Although when I give a ring in marriage or hand over the keys to a new incumbent, I am not merely moving a piece of gold or iron but pledging my own future actions and authorizing another's, yet we cannot really contrast the bodily behaviour with an inner significance it resembles but also differs from. In these cases the symbolism is, indeed, a natural one, but in most others it is purely conventional – as when I sign a cheque or nod my head in an auction. Significance, therefore, should not be seen as being necessarily contrasted with reality, since it does not require natural resemblance or congruence, but can rest on any convention provided it is sufficiently widely understood. For this reason, once the doctrine of the eucharist was established, the natural symbolism of eating and drinking could be supplemented – or even supplanted – by the traditional understanding of what the church was doing when it celebrated the eucharist; and the intense Paschal associations introduced *nuances* of meaning and modes of interpretation far beyond the natural symbolism of a shared meal. The description of what he did is given in terms of what his action meant, and we cannot contrast what he 'really' did with what it signified any more than I can contrast my signing a contract with some mysterious meaning of what I am doing. In actions, although not in things, the intention and the deed are inextricably bound up together, and from this it follows that we cannot talk of a bare deed apart from its intention, meaning or significance, and if those doing something intend it to mean something, then for them in that context it does. This is why many different understandings of the eucharist are possible, and perhaps valid, and why many different eucharistic practices have grown up. If one church believes the point of celebrating the eucharist to be the commemoration of our Lord's death, then that *is* what they are doing when they celebrate the eucharist, and if another believes it to be the vicarious offering by Christ's church of his passion to the Father, then that is what they are doing. Nevertheless, in spite of the great plasticity of meaning, not every interpretation is equally valid, nor every practice properly to be accounted eucharistic. The church rejects transubstantiation because it makes a thing of God. The chemical or pharmacological model is bad, because it depersonalizes the holy communion. Chemical substances can be manipulated and misused. It is quite reasonable to take uranium 235 to the field of battle, and expose one's enemies to its power. It does not matter for the efficiency of the penicillin I am taking that I have a whole-hearted acceptance of God's will for me. But God cannot be captured and localized in the host, and carted off to battle, and whosoever consumes the elements insincerely is not securing his own immortality but blaspheming. In a very different way, those who make of the eucharist a mere memorial of a past event are implicitly denying the continuing power of the cross for the present, and the fact of the resurrection. Some interpretations and practices are to be rejected because they say too much and would support conclusions repugnant to the Spirit of Christ: others because they say too little and leave unsecured saving truths of the Christian life: and others yet again because what they say is inconsistent either with itself or with other truths we have more reason to be confident of.

Nevertheless, although not all understandings of the eucharist are equally valid and some are to be rejected as altogether inadequate, we should be cautious in denying what we may regard as the erroneous opinions of others. The church has held differing opinions about New Testament scholarship, and what was in our Lord's mind when he instituted the eucharist. We cannot simply take over accounts of the eucharist based on what we regard as a misconception: but we should not automatically discard them as altogether mistaken. Christianity is a historical religion, and should treat with respect the various understandings of the eucharist that have been reached by different parts of the church in the course of its history. Although they are not all of equal value, few are without any value at all. And where they go wrong is usually in being pushed too far to the exclusion of other insights. Rather than reject them altogether, we should be disposed to accept them for what they are worth, but see the limits within which they can be usefully applied, recognizing that we shall always need a number of different accounts of what we are doing when we celebrate the eucharist, if we are to be faithful to the many different ways of understanding it which our Lord himself taught us.

2

Matter in the Theological and Scientific Perspectives – A Sacramental View

A. R. Peacocke

Although it has been common to decry from the pulpit the 'materialism' of our present age, meaning by this the current obsession with the material goods of life, it is easily overlooked that there is a sense in which the Christian faith is differentiated from other world religions by the realism of its attitude to the physical and biological character of man's existence. William Temple stressed this feature of Christian understanding in a striking passage: 'Christianity is the most materialistic of all great religions. The others hope to achieve spiritual reality by ignoring matter – calling it illusion (*maya*) or saying that it does not exist.... Christianity, based as it is on the Incarnation, regards matter as destined to be the vehicle and instrument of spirit, and spirit as fully actual as far as it controls and directs matter.'[1] The basis of this Christian materialism he grounds firmly in the doctrine of the incarnation: 'In the great affirmation that "the word became flesh and we beheld his glory" (John 1.14) is implicit a whole theory of the relation between spirit and matter.'[2] From the outset Christianity was anti-gnostic in its understanding of the material basis of men's life and its repudiation of a total otherworldliness.

However, there was a tendency amongst Christian thinkers in response to the Darwinian controversies to find their way out of the impasse then created by reverting to a naïve dualism in which the physical and biological world was assigned to science and that of 'mind' and 'spirit' to religion in general and Christianity in particular. This saved Christians from thinking too hard about the developing sciences and salved the consciences of the scientists who

Matter in the Theological and Scientific Perspectives

were thereby freed to get on with their work. This they did and the scientific and Christian communities continued, and still continue, to go their separate ways. Yet Christians should not have delegated to science all the responsibility for formulating ideas concerning the stuff, the matter, of the cosmos. For, as stressed by Temple, Christian teaching about the 'two natures' in the one 'person' of Jesus had profound implications about what was possible in the material universe which includes men's bodies and personalities. Moreover, by their character some of the central practices of the Christian faith predispose and point to, even if they do not logically compel, a certain way of regarding the material aspects of the cosmos. This applies particularly to its sacramental use of bread, wine and water.[3] In these sacramental communal acts of worship a particular significance is being attributed to these very material objects in a Christian context. Coherent with and, to some extent, implicit in this usage there is a teaching concerning the meaning to be attached to matter, the stuff of the cosmos – answers to the questions 'What is matter doing?', 'What is matter for?' For it is a generally recognized feature of a sacrament that it is something singled out and set apart, yet of a universal character. Hence we might reasonably hope that from an understanding of the significance of the Christian use of the matter of bread and wine in the eucharist, in particular, further insight into the meaning of the material cosmos might be derived. *Mutatis mutandis*, we might hope that light will be thrown on the meaning of the sacraments by our scientific understanding of the behaviour and potentialities of matter. It must be stressed that these hopes are not certain of fulfilment, but nevertheless it seems worth exploring, in the following two sections, possible answers to the two questions that have been implicitly posed: 'What is the rôle of the matter in a sacrament, in general, and in the eucharist in particular?' and 'How does the scientific perspective affect our understanding of matter?'

I *Matter in the Eucharist and other Christian Sacraments*

Men are accustomed in their mutual interactions to use material things in ways which both express their mind, or intentions, and which simultaneously effect what is in their mind, or fulfil their intentions. Thus a signed order form both expresses the desire of the one who signs it to purchase, say, a book and sets the sequence of events in motion which leads to his possessing it; a deed of covenant both expresses the mind and attitudes of benevolence of an individual to some project and itself contributes to the realization of that project. Analogously, in the Christian understanding of God's relation to physical reality, the world of matter is seen as both expressing and revealing the mind of God, its Creator, and as effecting his purposes. For the physical, material world which he has brought into existence is the matrix within which and the means whereby autonomous, personal agents can be brought into existence and into harmony and union with himself. Thus, in the Christian understanding, the world of matter, in its relation to God, has both the *symbolic* function of expressing his mind and the *instrumental* function of being the means whereby he effects his purpose. We could perhaps put it thus: the created world is seen by Christians as a symbol because it is a mode of God's revelation, an expression of his truth and beauty which are the 'spiritual' aspects of its reality;[4] it is also valued by them for what God is effecting instrumentally through it, what he does for men in and through it. But these two functions of matter, the symbolical and instrumental, also constitute the special character of the use of matter in the particular Christian sacraments.[5] Hence there is, in each particular sacrament, a universal reference to this double character of created physical reality and, correspondingly, meaning can be attached to speaking of the created world as a sacrament or, at least, as sacramental. However, it must be recognized that this sacramental character is only implicit, and that it is obscure and partial both because of man's limited perception and sensitivity and because of evil. The significance of the incarnation of God in a man within the created world is that in the incarnate Christ the sacramental character of that world was made explicit and perfected. In this sense, it seems legitimate to regard the incarnate life of Christ as the supreme sacrament. For in this outward historical life, there is both uniquely expressed and uniquely operative that purpose of goodness which is the purpose of God himself that all life and all nature should fulfil.

In the sacraments of the church, these two ultimate sacraments, the created order and Christ as God incarnate, regularly come together and are brought into one focus in time and place. At the Last Supper, which developed into the church's eucharist, Jesus identified the mode of his incarnation and reconciliation of God and man (his 'body and blood') with the very stuff of the universe when he took the bread, blessed, broke and gave it to his disciples saying,[6] 'This: my flesh for you', and similarly the wine, saying, 'This: my blood of the (new) covenant', or, in parallel to the other saying, and more simply, 'This: my blood for you (and for many)'. It seems to me that it is a legitimate extension and development of the ideas and symbolic references which are implicit in these features of this original historical act to affirm that, in this act, a new value was explicitly set upon the bread and wine, obstinately molecular as they are, an intimate part of the natural world (corn and grapes) and a product of men's co-operation with nature (bread and wine). His words and these acts seem to me to have involved a revaluation of the things themselves, a new value assigned by God himself in Christ. A further development seems natural in the light of what has been said above about the universal reference of sacramental acts: that to which a new value was imputed was not only these particular elements of bread and wine used in *this* way, but the whole created material world. For a sacrament has significance only as a part of a whole, of which the true relation to God is being represented and effectively realized.[7]

This value was implicit, though not available to man's observation, in the act of creation. It remained a potentiality of matter, only partially realized by man. It was the ground of the incarnation, the root of its possibility, for it was in his own world that God was incarnate in a man, that world of which he was already the formative principle. Even at the historic Last Supper, he was still largely incognito to his disciples, but to Christians he is now no longer unknown. So in Christian thinking the sacraments as a whole, especially the eucharist, manifest continually the ultimate meaning of matter as a symbol of God's being and as an instrument of his purpose.

The participants in the eucharist consciously and humbly offer their own lives in service to God and man in unity with the self-offered life of Christ which is believed to be present in and with the elements of bread and wine in the context of the total communal act. Thus, in this act, Christian believe they are participating in that re-formation and new creation of humanity which the coming of Jesus initiated through his incarnation and self-offering, cogently represented by the bread and wine offered with sacrificial reference both at the original Last Supper and at every eucharist of the church since then. This union with the offering of Christ is not self-directed, but 'for others', and it is worth noticing that what Christ took and what is used in the eucharist is the product of man's action on nature, bread not corn, wine not grapes. So the whole life and work of man may be regarded as offered in this act which is so closely associated with the historic initiation of the new humanity 'in Christ'. Many themes interlock and interweave in this central act of Christian worship, and all of these themes have immense significance for our attitude to the stuff of the cosmos of which we ourselves are part. It is interesting to note that the eucharist of the Christian church which, like a parabolic mirror, focusses so many parallel rays into one point of time and space, from the earliest times contained overt references to God's creative activity, although this insight has been somewhat obscured since then. For the 'words of institution' of Jesus, already referred to, took place within the context of the Jewish meal-time blessings over bread and wine (the 'cup of blessing'). These blessings took the form of a thanksgiving to God for creation.[8] Similarly directed thanksgivings appear in the earliest liturgies of the church's eucharist[9] and are referred to by Irenaeus (c. AD 130-c. 200) whose words are worth quoting more fully.[10] He speaks of Jesus as:

> Instructing his disciples to offer to God the first-fruits of his own creation, not as though he had need of them, but, that they themselves might be neither unfruitful nor ungrateful. He took that bread which comes of the [material] creation and gave thanks saying, This is my body. And the cup likewise, which is [taken] from created things, like ourselves, he acknowledged for his own blood, and taught the new oblation of the New Covenant ... we ought to make oblation to God ... offering first fruits of those things which are his creatures.

These prayers of thanksgiving in the eucharist developed naturally into an offertory of other foods, in addition to bread and wine. In the course of a complex history this basic feature has been fragmented and overlaid, but still survives in the '... these thy *creatures* of bread and wine ...' in Holy Communion in the Book of Common Prayer of the Church of England and in the '... *haec dona, haec munera, haec sancta sacrificia illibata* ...' of the traditional Latin Mass.

II *Matter in the Scientific Perspective – From the Inorganic to the Personal*

The ability of human beings to survey their surroundings as subjects, to regard everything other than themselves as objects of their own consciousness, and so, as it were, to transcend the world, has long dominated men's view of themselves. Men have tended, and still do so, to regard their surroundings as a kind of stage on which their own personal drama is enacted, themselves in the foreground. This natural, everyday approach to the external features of man's life has played, in a variety of sophisticated forms, a dominant rôle in his reflections on his own nature and destiny. But in the last hundred years the perspective of the sciences concerned with the origin and development of the physical and biological worlds has altered this outlook in a way which is, or should be, changing profoundly the way man is coming to regard himself. Our familiar environments of stone, water, air, earth, grass, birds, animals and so on are seen both to share with us common molecular structures and to be stages in a common development in time. The very stuff of which we are made and the way it has become organized as ourselves is an inherent part of the ongoing development of the physical cosmos which we survey. We, and all other living creatures, have emerged in time out of the non-living world of water, air and rocks which seem so distinct and different from us.

Although this continuity of man with the organic world had sometimes been accepted in principle (e.g. Gen. 2.7: 'And the Lord God formed man out of the dust of the ground and breathed into his nostrils the breath of life; and man became a living soul'), it was not until about a hundred years ago that the scientific evidence of man's relation to other species began to appear, and it is only in the last few decades that the emergence of primitive living organisms from inorganic matter could be delineated in any fashion which had a scientific basis. This knowledge of biological evolution and of molecular biology, together with the new insights into the development of the physical cosmos which the astrophysicists and geologists are obtaining, now transpose the intimations of the writers in Genesis into the realm of well-supported scientific inference.

It is the purpose of this present section[11] to outline briefly this sequence of development, and to delineate some of its characteristic features so that the scientific perspective on matter may be set alongside and compared with the implications discerned above in Christian sacramental practice and theology. Many of the developments described are past and are now inevitably no longer available for observation (except those occurring in galaxies many light-years distant from us). However, and this is what characterizes the present position as distinct from previous speculations, the inferences now made about these long-past developments and processes are reasonable extrapolations from changes and processes which we can observe now. So the perspective which unfolds can be described as genuinely scientific and even if in many respects it has to be revised (especially with respect to the development of the galaxies and the way in which primitive forms of life first emerged in an inorganic matrix), the fact of such developments and their continuity from the primordial sub-atomic particles to man can now be said to rest on a basis of well-established scientific observations and concepts.

The Cosmic Development

Hydrogen appears to be the basic material out of which the universe is 'built', and its atoms, which are the simplest and occur throughout the universe, each consist of a heavy, positively charged, nucleus (proton) and a much lighter, negatively charged, electron distributed around it. More complex atoms contain in their nucleus not only protons but also neutrons, of the same mass and no charge, to a total number of as much as 250 with the central positive charge balanced by extra-nuclear electrons whose arrangements and energies govern the combination between atoms to form molecules. In order to understand why the nuclei of atoms hold together, and with such tremendous forces, it has become necessary to postulate the existence of a whole new 'world' of over a hundred sub-nuclear particles, many of which have subsequently been detected by the breakdown of the nuclei in high-energy accelerators. The symmetry and other rules which relate these sub-nuclear particles continue to constitute a major conceptual problem in modern physics and serve to stress how little we understand of what matter is 'in itself'.

Atoms can combine to form molecules with energies about ten to a hundred times smaller than those which hold the electrons in the atoms (which are themselves orders of magnitude smaller than those holding the nucleus together): even so, the forces holding atoms together in molecules are still of the order of 10^{30} greater than the gravitational attractions between them. Molecules exert weak forces on each other which hold them together in solids and liquids, even when they possess no net charge, and quantitative accounts can be given of the opposition between the tendency to reach a minimum energy and the tendency to achieve the maximum possible number of ways of distributing a given energy. With matter in bulk of a terrestrial order, and with planets and astronomical bodies, the relatively weak gravitational and magnetic forces become highly significant.

The Earth moves round and receives its energy from its 'star', the Sun, in which the energy is produced by the reaction of hydrogen nuclei to form helium nuclei. The Sun, which consists mainly of hydrogen, has existed for about 5,000 million years and is one of c. 10^{11} stars in the universe.[12] The universe contains a great variety of different kinds of bodies at different stages of development and whose distances are such that they are now being observed as they were aeons ago. Study of their electro-magnetic radiation over the whole spectrum has, especially in the last few decades, enabled astrophysicists and astronomers to understand the nature of the transformation of matter taking place in many of these bodies and to discern the development of the physical cosmos with more assurance than ever before.

Whatever the mode of formation of galaxies[13] from whirling masses of hydrogen atoms, and the processes of internal coalescence and eddying which they underwent, it seems that our galaxy (containing the Sun, and so the Earth) came into existence about 15,000 million years ago and the sun about 10,000 million years later. The inner planets of the solar system, Mercury, Venus, Mars and the earth, condensed out of the heavier elements within this primordial sun about 4,500 million years ago. The Earth possessed at this stage an atmosphere like that of Jupiter now which consisted of methane, hydrogen, ammonia, hydrogen cyanide and sulphide, as well as water: its crust contained water and metal silicates and carbides. Chemical experiments in the last ten years have shown *inter alia* how such an atmosphere, subject to the intense light of the sun and to lightning, and in contact with water, could give rise to those molecular structures – nucleic acid bases, amino acids, sugars – which are necessary precursors of any form of living matter. For the first 1500 million years of its existence these compounds must have been gradually accumulating on the earth and becoming concentrated in particular localities. They are the building blocks of the big molecules ('macromolecules' – proteins and nucleic acids) which are essential to life[14] or, more precisely, to matter which has the characteristics we call living, that is, the ability to self-produce, to maintain highly-ordered structures at the expense of the energy of other molecules, to grow, to develop in time, etc. The nucleic acids transmit the genetic 'blueprint' of living organisms, and the proteins act as specific catalysts for biological chemical processes, as carriers of small molecules, as structural materials and in many other important ways. There is much discussion[15] about which kind of macromolecules came first, but the essential point is that reasonable postulates can now be made on the basis of the mutual interconnections in control and catalysis of these two macromolecules, relationships which have only become known in the last fifteen years.

The original reproducing aggregates of macromolecules must have coagulated and acquired a membrane at some point; at each stage they would not have been prey to bacteria and other organisms which today would feed on any such molecular complexes, since no such other living organisms were then present. At some point, a number of such 'proto-cells' must have come into existence and have competed for limited sources of 'food' (i.e. simpler molecules), and so a process of competitive selection would then have begun to operate. The development of a photosynthetic mechanism (which changes carbon dioxide to oxygen by means of light) must have occurred approximately 3,000 million years ago and so initiated the building up of oxygen in the earth's atmosphere. It then became advantageous for another type of cell to utilize plant compounds for energy and for building materials, in some cases oxidizing them with the increasing atmospheric oxygen. So one of the early great divergences in life began, about 600 million years ago, in the phase called pre-Cambrian.

In the period c. 500 to 570 million years ago, when the Cambrian rocks were being laid down, fairly advanced representatives of the main phyla, but not the true vertebrates, of the animal kingdom came into existence. From then on, development of living organisms breaks up into many branching lines, some continuing until the present, others terminating long ago. The unravelling of this complex story is the outcome of patient comparisons of structures, functions, habitats and of the behaviour of living and fossil creatures, and was a magnificent intellectual achievement, long before the discoveries of *molecular* biology. Some idea of the complexity can be gained when one realizes that there are over a million extant known species of living creatures (excluding varieties within them), and these constitute only a small fraction of those known to have existed in the past. The sequence of biological evolution is recalled in outline in the Appendix, which mentions only some of the major types appearing at different stages and does no justice at all either to the immense development of species already present or the numerous lines which have come to an end. Even so, the sequence indicates the increasingly rapid development of life with time, and the relatively recent appearance of man.

How did this remarkable development occur? The basic principles were formulated by Darwin and Wallace over a hundred years ago and, although they knew nothing of modern genetics and molecular biology, their basic insight is now generally accepted, though with many modifications and amplifications. Their main contention was that it was populations of organisms, not individual organisms, which evolved, and that they did so because of 'natural selection'. This term was used for the statistically greater chance of those creatures surviving to produce progeny which had, through variations, some advantage in the struggle for life – for limited food sources, with each other, against climatic changes, and so on. These progeny would inherit these variations and so form a new 'norm' with respect to which further variations, favourable and unfavourable to survival, could then occur. The whole context of discussion of this fundamental idea has been deepened and sharpened by our knowledge of the mechanism of inheritance in its statistical and cellular and molecular aspects. The statistical genetic 'factors' are located in the deoxyribonucleic acid (DNA) and the chromosomes. These 'factors', or genes, are subject to sudden changes, mutations, as a result of structural changes in the DNA, which are probably the result of irradiation processes or chemical events and which are random with respect to the biological needs of the organism. The process of natural selection favours the survival of those which help the organism in its competitive life. Many different forms of selection process are now distinguished, and the complexities and subtleties (which are greater than seemed likely fifty years ago) of the interplay of heredity, environment, mutations, variation and behaviour are still being disentangled. For our present purposes it is enough to note that the development is regarded as proceeding by statistical laws which express the regularity of the biological effects of apparently random molecular events, and that there is within the immense diversity of living forms a unity of structures, especially at the molecular level, and a continuity with simpler past forms.

Distinctive Features of the Process

The process just outlined may be called 'evolutionary' in the strict dictionary sense of referring to 'an appearance (of events etc.) in due succession' (OED) and, provided we are not misled into reading into the term any dominant theological or other implication, the process may be properly called 'cosmic' – again in the strict sense of referring to the cosmos, by which we mean all-that-is insofar as it has been possible to view it as an ordered whole. Hence, I will use the term 'cosmic evolution' or 'cosmic development' to refer to the whole sequence just outlined but not intending thereby to make any judgment in advance of an examination of the character of this process as it emerges from the various kinds of scientific enquiry. These features may be summarized as follows:

(i) *Continuity*. The whole of the present variety of living organisms, and of all those species long since extinct, can be traced back in a continuous line to those one or few ordered aggregates of molecules which first acquired the ability to replicate themselves and to grow by incorporating surrounding molecules. This continuity with a simpler molecular form can also be traced back in the life of the present individual to the relatively few molecules of DNA which it inherited from its precursor(s). In one sense we share with all living organisms not only a common origin in the 'primeval soup' in which life first appeared but also a common kind of 'molecular' parenthood, insofar as all living creatures begin their existence as one or a small number of molecules of DNA. Not surprisingly, we share with many living organisms common molecular processes whereby, *inter alia*, we store and utilize energy, make mechanical movements, see light, move substances across membranes, etc.

A thoroughgoing 'materialistic' view of our existence and of that of all living organisms is apparently justified if, and only if, it is qualified by the recognition that the most significant of the properties of 'matter' is that organized in certain ways it can have the characteristics we call living and human. The primordial nebular cloud of hydrogen – or of its subnuclear 'particulate' predecessors – has developed into living organisms and into man, with all his special qualities, achievements and potentialities for sublimity and degradation. If we are prepared to recognize that matter, the stuff of the universe, has this character, and that the continuity I have described is from hydrogen atoms to the personalities and creative genius of men at their most developed, then it is still legitimate to call the process 'materialistic'. However, my guess is that, for most of us, the term 'matter' is so firmly tied down to the Newtonian conceptual scheme, with most non-scientists taking little or no account of the revolutionary concepts of quantum and relativity theory, that it will prove to be an inadequate term. We really need some new label for the stuff of the universe to denote not only its most broken-down, 'ultimate' form as atoms and sub-nuclear particles, but also its most developed forms in the living world and notably in man himself.

(ii) *By natural 'laws'*. Each transition within the cosmic development can be seen, in the light of our present-day scientific knowledge, to proceed in accordance with regularities in parallel observations we can make in or infer from our present experimental and theoretical investigation of the world we know. Briefly, we can say the cosmic development has proceeded by natural 'law', at the same time recognizing the considerable discussion which this term has evoked. It is used here simply to denote the ordered and regular character of the knowledge which scientific investigation yields by the methodologies it has established, and which have been so powerfully vindicated, in the last three hundred years. Alternatively, one could say that this development is within the 'nomological net', i.e. the system of scientific concepts and laws.[16]

Even though biological evolution is based on the natural selection of mutations which occur at random with respect to the biological needs of an individual organism, it can no more be said to occur 'by chance' than can those properties of gases which are the statistical summation of the effects of a very large number of random collisions between their constituent molecules. Indeed the vast majority of scientific observations are statistical in this sense. Thus biological evolution no more qualifies for description as a 'chance' process than any other. There is, nevertheless, a particularity about biological evolution, since once a variation has been favoured in an organism in a habitat in a particular location, the future variations which will then be favourable to that organism will be the result of the interplay of these variations past and present with the climatic and other factors (including other creatures) in that particular environment. The imprinting of the new variation yields gains in viability at the expense of channelling and limiting future possibilities.

(iii) *Emergence and creativity*. The cosmic development is apparently a process in which new forms of organization of matter appear at successive times and in which at each stage these new forms represent new collations and spatial and temporal organizations of simpler units whose earlier appearance on the scene are the prior condition for the new forms to emerge. The word 'emergent' is often used to denote also the difficulty of fully explaining the mode of being of the newly-appearing form in terms of its immediate, and even more so its distant, predecessors. The new 'wholes' are not, it is claimed, reducible or describable entirely in terms of the former 'parts'. It is important to realize that it is reasonable to affirm and recognize this emergent character of the cosmic development, as for example Polanyi[17] does, without thereby intending to postulate in any sense any special super-added force or principle ('elan vital', 'entelechy', 'life force') which somehow mysteriously distinguishes living organisms from their non-living components. For the principle applies equally to the logical impossibility of reducing the principles of operation of, for example, a steam engine to the physics and chemistry of each of its components considered separately. The principles of mechanical engineering, of the organizations of matter in space and time, which elaborate the different categories and delineate the effectiveness (etc.) of engines, are not the same as those of the physics and chemistry which properly describe the general properties of steel, water and carbon and the processes of combustion and gaseous expansion, all of which are integrated to constitute an engine.

New properties of matter, its functions and abilities, have genuinely emerged in the successive stages of the cosmic development, and this may now be taken as a datum of our thinking. The laws, principles and categories of thinking and vocabulary needed to describe each stage of this process will be particular to and characteristic of it. In this sense, chemistry is not 'nothing-but' physics, especially the physics of the nucleus; nor is biology 'nothing-but' physics and chemistry; nor is human psychology and sociology 'nothing-but' biology. All these ascriptions, which aspire to subsume the more developed form in terms of the intellectual concepts and experimental approaches which have succeeded at the lower and especially the immediately preceeding levels, constitute a mistaken analysis of the modes of investigation which each level of organization of matter renders necessary for its understanding.[18]

Given, then, that in the cosmic development new forms and organizations of matter genuinely emerge, it does not seem to me to be inappropriate to describe this development as 'creative', by analogy with human creativity as observed externally. For the observer of human creativity would note that previously unrelated sounds, words, ideas, materials, events and so on are, by the human creative artist, juxtaposed in new arrangements in space and time that, taken together, then have a form which gives them a new meaning and sense and which had previously not existed in that way. The imaginative processes by which human beings create forms are, no doubt, very different from the processes by which new material forms have emerged in the cosmic development. But both, viewed as it were from outside, can be properly called 'creative', for something new emerges in both. Curiously enough, there is also another sense in which both kinds of creation of the newly emergent, the human and the cosmic, are similar; for both, it seems, run the risk of failure and exhibit continually renewed attempts at new constructions.

(iv) *Directions in evolution*. There is a natural tendency to see the whole cosmic development as a process leading to ourselves. This could be but a new form of the anthropomorphism which in earlier centuries placed man on his earth at the centre of the cosmos; now we tend to place him at the pinnacle of the time-scale of cosmic development. The first was shown to be wrong by scientific observations, but the second has a basis in fact, for man is indeed one of the last of living organisms to emerge and does have unique characteristics, as we shall see. But it is essential first to examine biological development as objectively as possible to ascertain what trends can be discerned, discounting, as far as one can, the fact that it is men who are themselves surveying this development. In making this examination we can do no better than to follow the discussion of G. G. Simpson,[19] who cannot be accused of any 'supernaturalist' bias and who, in *The Meaning of Evolution*, is attempting an assessment of the kind we need at this stage. Simpson discerns, *inter alia*, the following trends in biological evolution: a tendency for living organisms to expand to fill all available spaces in the liveable environments; a succession of dominant types in biological evolution (leading to description of periods in the earth's history as the 'Age of Fishes', the 'Age of Amphibia', etc.), but with no one single line of dominant types; a successive invasion and development of environmental and adaptive spheres; an increasing specialization with its corollary of improvement in efficiency and adaptability, though these two features may at times be in conflict with each other; an apparent tendency to increase in complexity, although it is extremely hard[20] to obtain any objective criterion of complexity once one begins to compare the higher mammals with each other rather than, say, a fish with an amoeba; an increasing tendency for reproduction to be protected and towards an increasing care of the young; an increased awareness of the environment, in the sense of ability to react appropriately to it;[21] an increasing independence in each individual organism as a unit, with distinctive and individual reactions and relationships.

So biological evolution as a whole is accompanied by movement in many directions, no one of which can be described as towards a single perfect form. Yet all the biological criteria, except the succession of dominant types and specialization (for which man more than compensates by his extreme adaptability), place man at a level at which the trends in question reach their maximum expression – that is, in wider usage, their 'highest' development. Man stands at a uniquely high point in evolution with respect to all criteria, except the third and fourth, and he is unique in his adaptability, individualization and (I would add) his intelligence, socialization and use of language. Simpson concludes: 'Man is among the highest products of evolution and a balance of them [the criteria] warrants the conclusion that man is, on the whole, but not in every single respect, the pinnacle so far of evolutionary progress.'[22] It is clearly, as Polanyi affirms,[23] a false modesty, verging on intellectual perversity, to 'renounce, in the name of scientific objectivity, our position as the highest form of life on earth and our own advent by a process of evolution as the most important problem of evolution'.

Of the trends in biological evolution which have been identified in the preceding discussion, only two seem also to be applicable to the pre-biological developments: the increase in complexity and an increase in individualization. The complexity criterion is in this context more clear-cut and convincing. For each successive aggregation and coalescence of matter, as the cosmic development has preceded, has clearly led to more complex forms assembled from simpler units.

Man in the Universe

If we are to interpret the whole cosmic development honestly, then we are bound to look at all the facts. The presence of man in the universe is just such a fact – the fact of the emergence in the cosmos of the new features and properties of matter which appear when it is organized in the form we call man. Briefly, with man evolution has become 'history', for man shapes his own physical environment and intellectual and cultural inheritance by his own choices based on his own inner drives and values which determine how he applies his unique awareness of that environment. Sir Julian Huxley calls this form of evolution 'psycho-social' although, as hinted above, the term 'history' is available for use in this sense.[24]

The new features and behaviour which have emerged in man

within the cosmic development can only be described by their own appropriate language and concepts, and necessitate modes of enquiry peculiar to themselves. There are thus no grounds for rejecting, on a supposedly scientific basis, those words and modes of speaking which men have developed to describe the uniquely human experience of the world and of their understanding of themselves and their mutual relationships. Thus the language of personal relationships, of the terms used to denote intellectual and aesthetic activities, the nature of the consciousness viewed from within, and all these and many more are as legitimately applied to describe and understand human beings as the language of chemistry for molecules, of physiology for the inter-relation between organs in living creatures, of ethology for animal behaviour and so on. This is not to say such language will not need to be refined and clarified, but the fact of its existence and the existence of the human experience which has evoked its formation are part of the givenness of the cosmic development and cannot be ignored in any account of the cosmos which claims scientific objectivity. For the stuff of the world, the primeval concourse of hydrogen atoms or sub-nuclear particles, has as a matter of fact, and not conjecture, become man who possesses not only a social life and biological organization but also an inner life in relation to others, that which makes him personal. How are we properly to speak of the cosmic development if after aeons of time the atoms have become human beings, persons? Paradoxically, knowledge of the process by which they have arrived in the world seems to be confined to human beings. We alone reflect on our atomic and simpler forbears and we alone adjust our behaviour in the light of this perspective.

To ignore the glory, the predicament and the possibilities of man in assessing the trend and meaning of the cosmic development would be as unscientific as to endorse the former pre-Copernican account of the universe which was based on the contrary prejudice. Apparently, developing under the control of the regular processes of natural laws, new forms of matter have creatively emerged out of the nuclear particles and atoms of several thousand million years ago and have now in man become conscious both of the processes by which they have been brought into existence and of themselves. From man's consciousness new creativities of a specifically human kind have erupted, notably in men of genius but, equally significantly, in the very real individual creativity of each human being within his own social environment which, however humble, far transcends that of the highest animal. The presence of man and the fact of human personalness is therefore part of the givenness of the developing cosmos which science has unfolded.

III *A Sacramental View of the Cosmos*

In discussing the continuity of the cosmic development, it was suggested that we need to revise what we mean by 'matter' and its associated adjective 'materialistic'. For just as the wetness of water, or the viscosity of a nucleic acid solution, are not properties of their constituent atoms but features of their higher molecular and macromolecular levels of organization, so the properties and behaviour of living organisms can be regarded as manifestations of the potentialities of matter if incorporated into certain organized structures. How such incorporation can come about and how the 'boundary conditions' of the structures are established are problems to which we have adverted already. However, once they are established, each level of organization displays its characteristic features. To be consistent, one would say that matter organized in the way we call man, notably, of course, in the labyrinth which constitutes his brain, is capable of activities which we describe as those of conscious thought, of self-reflection (self-consciousness), of communication with other human beings, and all the inter-relations of personal life and ethical behaviour, of creativity in art and science and, indeed, of all the activities individual and social which characterize and differentiate man from the rest of the biological world. At each emergent level in evolution, matter in its newly evolved mode of organization manifests properties which could not, in principle, be discerned in the earlier levels from which the new emerges. In a sense, therefore, one could say that the potentialities of matter have been, and still are being, realized in the cosmic development. However, matter has evolved into man and it seems we cannot avoid concluding, even from the most materialistic viewpoint, that the culmination of evolution in man demonstrates the ability of matter (a long-hidden potentiality now realized) to display in man functions and properties for which we have to use special terms such as 'mental', 'personal', 'spiritual'. We have to employ these special terms (which cannot, without gross qualification, be transferred even to the higher mammals) because these properties, emergent in man, are uniquely and characteristically human. Such an affirmation of, for example, the reality of human conscious and self-conscious activities, is not dependent on any

Matter in the Theological and Scientific Perspectives 31

particular philosophy of the relation of an entity called 'mind' to one called 'body'. This problem remains open, on this view, to philosophical analysis: it is the fact that the problem arises and can be posed on which attention is here being focussed. For it seems that by taking seriously the scientific perspective, we cannot avoid arriving at a view of matter which sees it as manifesting mental, personal and spiritual activities. If we were unashamedly metaphysical and were to regard these qualities as pertaining to a different mode of existence, we might reasonably describe matter as the vehicle or means of expression of this mental, personal and spiritual mode. However, whether or not we adopt this more metaphysical view of mind, persons and spirit, there is a real convergence between the implication of the scientific perspective on the capabilities of matter and the sacramental view of matter which Christians have adopted as the natural consequence of the meaning they attach to Jesus's life and the continued existence of the church. For, as explained above, Christians have had to understand matter both in the light of their conviction that matter was able in the man Jesus to express the being of God, who is nevertheless regarded as supra-mental, supra-personal and supra-spiritual, so that his mode of being lies beyond any sequence of mental, etc., superlatives we can delineate; and in the light of their understanding of the sacramental acts of Jesus, made in the context of his death and resurrection, and in which the continuing life of Christian humanity originates. Briefly, it looks as if Christians, starting, as it were, from one end with their experience of God in Christ through the Holy Spirit acting in the stuff of the world, have developed an insight into matter which is consonant with that which is now evoked by the scientific perspective working from matter towards man, and beyond.

This congruence, for which I argue, between the perspective of the cosmos which science has developed and the Christian understanding of God's cosmic purposes as expressed ('symbolically') and effected ('instrumentally') through nature, the incarnation and the eucharist is not meant to imply any identity in the way they impress themselves on us – even within the terms of Christian discourse. For science is *par excellence* a human activity of ratiocination based on experimental, empirical observations; while, for the Christian, there is a certain givenness about our encounter with God in Christ in the eucharist which cannot finally be subsumed under purely human, psychological terms. This givenness of the eucharist is quite distinctive but, it is urged, it is also reasonable by virtue of its congruence with the scientific perspective. The nature of this givenness of God in Christ in the eucharist can tentatively be elaborated, in terms akin to those used earlier in discussing the cosmic development, as follows. In the eucharist, a conjunction occurs of a group of baptized Christians, who are committed to fulfilling God's purposes in the world and who are consciously acting corporately in communion with each other, with the elements of bread and wine which are present because of their historical continuity with the Last Supper of Jesus. We thus have in such events unique, though temporary, configurations of Christian man in relation to other Christian men and of bread and wine taken, blessed, broken and given because of the presumed intention of the historical Jesus. The assertion that God gives himself uniquely to men in this situation can be expressed as the assertion that in this unique configuration there emerges, in accordance with the divine purpose, a new potentiality of the stuff of the universe – just as it has in all the previous stages of the cosmic development, except that here it is mediated to men through the historic Christ – and that this new potentiality is characterized by God being able to act in and through this corporate event in ways denoted by such terms, *inter alia*, as 'presence' and 'sacrifice' as elaborated by other essays in this volume.

This way of looking at and speaking of the eucharist can, of its very nature, be only tentative, but what is clear is that there can be a mutual enrichment of Christian incarnational and sacramental insights by the scientific perspective and *vice versa*. Each approach remains distinctive and autonomous, but the relationship developed above indicates at least the possibility of convergence into a new unified vision, even if the parallel lines converge only at the infinity of the divine. This approach gives a new relevance to Christian sacramental worship which is now seen not to be representing some magical, cabbalistic and esoteric doctrine, but expressing, in a communal context, the basic nature of the cosmic process which has brought man to this point and in which he is now invited by his Creator to participate consciously and willingly.

A summary of this sacramental view,[25] which incorporates the Christian understanding of God's trinity of being and which takes seriously the scientific perspective, might be expressed thus. The world is created and sustained in being by the will of God, the will of perfect Love. The Son, the Logos, is the all-sufficient principle and form of this created order. At every level, this order reflects in its own measure something of the quality of deity. 'From atom and molecule to mammal and man, each by its appropriate order and function expresses the design inherent in it, and contributes, so far as it can by failure or success, to the fulfilment of the purpose.'[26] The continuing creative power which is manifest as a *nisus* at all levels of existence to attain its intended form is the Holy Spirit himself.

The process of creation has been unfolded by the natural sciences as one in which new qualities and modes of existence continuously emerge out of simpler forms of matter by the operation of natural laws. The newer forms depend for their existence on the regularity of behaviour of the simpler entities out of which they are constructed but manifest properties and activities which are specific to that level of organization of matter. The level of organization which is reached in man represents not only a new summit in this evolutionary process but a new departure in the way in which change is initiated. For the mode of organization which constitutes man is characterized by activities and purposes which are only describable in terms of mind and self-consciousness. What appear to be freely-willed decisions determine how the individual and society develop and how they alter their environment, which then interacts on each succeeding generation. By his intelligent apprehensions of his environment, man has become the controller and arbiter of the future of other forms of matter. He is nevertheless incomplete and unfulfilled and is tragically aware of the lack of fulfilment of his own potentialities. Thus it can be said that in man matter has become aware of itself, of its past, and of its unfulfilled potentialities.

The Christian claim, and here it differentiates itself from secular 'humanism', then amounts to the affirmation that this whole process is the outworking of the creative being of God in the world and goes on to assert further that this process has culminated in the manifestation of God as a man within the created world.[27] Only in a perfect man could God express explicitly his character as creative Love: all other levels of created being up to this point were inadequate for this purpose and but implicit manifestations of a God still *incognito*. Thus, on the one hand that which God has brought into existence, the stuff of the cosmos, is seen through the sciences to be the matrix and necessary condition for the appearance of purpose, mind, self-consciousness and values – all that characterizes the human person; and, on the other hand, the Christian revelation affirms that this character of the stuff of the cosmos is so fundamental that God expressed his being in, and acted through, the perfect culmination of this process in the person of Jesus of Nazareth. Indeed, in Jesus we really see what personalness amounts to. The two enterprises converge in a view of the cosmos which can therefore be properly called 'sacramental'. This technical theological term may be uncongenial to some (and not only to agnostics), but none other seems to be available which expresses so succinctly the simultaneous recognition of both the duality in our experiences represented by our familiar body-mind, subjective-objective, etc., dichotomies and the observed fact, in our own experience and in the evolutionary development revealed by the sciences, that all the 'higher' qualities of existence which characterize personal and mental life are qualities of matter in particular forms and *only* appear when matter is so organized. The term recognizes bluntly the duality necessary in our talk about themselves and about the character of the evolutionary process, but also recognizes that the mental and spiritual features of existence are always features of, and only of, the organized matter which constitutes the observable cosmos. It is not pretended that description of the cosmos as 'sacramental' represents any real solution of the body-mind and related problems. Nevertheless, the use of this term not only avoids both idealism and the grosser forms of materialism (in the old sense) but also serves to stress the consonance between the scientific understanding of the nature of man and what Christians think is revealed of nature, man and God through the life and actions of Jesus, himself the culmination of that historical process which was at work in the Hebraic culture and which has been attested in its literature.

At the historical crisis of the human life of the Jesus who was God incarnate, at the moment before 'the love which moves the sun and all stars' culminated in the self-offering of the cross, Jesus himself gave a new significance to that characteristic act of man's creaturehood, his need to imbibe the world of matter in order to live. Eventually, that common meal became the symbolic meal of the new humanity stemming from Christ, one might almost say of a new level of evolution of human potentialities. For the church believes that in the eucharist God acts to re-create both the individual man and society, to bring to fruition the purpose of his creation, manifest in the incarnation. In the eucharist, God expresses the significance of the created material order, and through it he is achieving his purpose for that order of protons, atoms, molecules, proteins, amoeba, mammals and man.

The eucharist focusses and summarizes the sacramental character of the whole of existence and thereby enhances our appreciation of that character; it does not subtract from it. Thus in the eucharist is expressed the Christian understanding of *all* human activity, which is in accordance with God's creative purposes, as the end of man and as man's proper fulfilment. The eucharist is then the concentrated expression of what the whole of life is about, not just the specifically 'religiously' oriented moments. The eucharist stands as a regular expression of the life-affirming character of the Christian faith, of a Christian humanism which stems from the fact that God has, *per impossibile*, expressed himself in and through an actual, historical human individual, whose human nature is itself the outcome of the evolution of matter. While it expresses the sacramental character of the whole of human life as it fulfils God's purposes, the eucharist also links this understanding with the historical life, death and resurrection of the man Jesus and their significance for all men. The perfect human life with which the Christian identifies himself by participating in the eucharist is the self-offered life of the 'man for others'. The eucharist is therefore not only fully human in its reference but also utterly and uniquely Christ-centred and God-given.

APPENDIX

Millions of years ago	Dominant and newly-appearing organisms
570–500	Calcareous fossils (crustaceans, molluscs, worms, echinoderms)
500–430	First vertebrates (fishes)
430–395	First known land plants, air-breathing animals, fishes numerous
395–345	Early land plants, amphibians, fishes dominant
354–280	Reptiles, insects, one type of plant (gymnosperms)
280–225	Conifers, land vertebrates
225–190	First mammals and dinosaurs
190–135	First flowering plants, primitive birds, flying reptiles, dinosaurs and insects
135– 65	More primitive mammals
65– 26	Modern mammals, anthropoid apes, more birds
26– 2	Man's remote ancestors, hominidae

Thousands of years ago	Predecessors of man
1,000–500	Australopithecus
500–200	Pithecanthropus
60– 40	Neanderthal man
40	*Homo Sapiens*

NOTES

1. William Temple, *Readings in St John's Gospel*, Macmillan 1955, pp.xx-xxi.
2. Op. cit., p.xx.
3. Technically, these have been denoted as the 'matter' which constitutes the appropriate sacrament in contrast to its particular 'form' and intention – but in the present discussion 'matter' refers to physical reality at various levels of complexity. (The word is notoriously ambiguous, and it is always important to be clear with what it is being contrasted.)
4. Cf. William Temple, *Nature, Man and God,* Macmillan 1934, ch.IV.
5. Cf. O. C. Quick, *The Christian Sacraments,* Nisbet ⁴1932.
6. There has been much investigation of what is the most authentic account of what Jesus actually said over the bread and the cup. What is quoted represents a common convergence of several such studies; all agree that, as there is no Aramaic word for 'is', it is justifiable to insert the break indicated by the colon (for further discussion see e.g. J. Jeremias, *The Eucharistic Words of Jesus*, SCM Press ²1966; J. A. Baker, The *Foolishness of God*, Darton, Longman and Todd 1970, pp.233f.).
7. Following Quick, op. cit., p.105.
8. Probably the word over the bread was very close to the form of the present Hebrew prayer book: 'Blessed art Thou, O Lord our God, King of the Universe, who bringest forth bread from the earth.' This is the pattern followed in the new Roman Catholic *missa normativa.*
9. See G. Dix, *The Shape of the Liturgy*, Dacre Press 1945.
10. From Dix, op. cit., pp.113f. (Irenaeus, *Adv. Haer.* IV, 17-18.6). It is not suggested, of course, that Irenaeus, in using such 'first-fruits' terminology, had adopted the view developed here. No doubt he was much more concerned with parallels between certain biblical texts. However, it is suggested that this feature of the eucharist of the early church to which he refers does in fact represent a genuine insight and point of growth for a legitimate further development.
11. A fuller account for the general reader is given in A. R. Peacocke, *Science and the Christian Experiment,* Oxford University Press 1971, which elaborates the approach adopted here. Extracts from pp.178, 180-2, 185-8 of that book are used here by permission.
12. These figures represent only orders of magnitude and are not precise.
13. See, for example, F. Hoyle, *The Nature of the Universe*, Blackwell 1966.
14. See, for example, A. R. Peacocke, 'The Molecular Organization of Life,' in I. T. Ramsey, *Biology and Personality*, Blackwell 1955, pp.17ff.
15. See, for example, J. D. Bernal, *The Origin of Life*, Weidenfeld and Nicholson 1967; M. Calvin, *Chemical Evolution*, Oxford University Press 1969; A. I. Oparin, *The Origin of Life on the Earth*, Pergamon Press 1959; other references are to be found in A. R. Peacocke, *Science and the Christian Experiment,* Appendix B.
16. H. Feigl, *The 'Mental' and the 'Physical'*, University of Minnesota Press 1967, p.66.
17. M. Polanyi, *Personal Knowledge,* Routledge and Kegan Paul 1958.

18. I suspect that, just as some 'vitalists' have been concerned to postulate externally added influences to 'explain' living organisms in the supposed and (I believe) mistaken interest of a non-materialistic view of existence, so many 'mechanists' have been impelled to claim biology as nothing-but-physics-and-chemistry, doing so on behalf of the opposite, supposedly materialistic view. The first view flies in the face of the evidence and the second fails to recognize that even a mechanism has its irreducible principles of organization which are *sui generis* and that the 'matter' to which the adjective 'materialist' is referring must, as mentioned earlier, now be recognized as having properties in its higher level of organization to which other vocabularies have been formerly and properly, applied (e.g. intelligence, drive, will, mind – spirit, even, in man).

19. G. G. Simpson, *The Meaning of Evolution*, Oxford University Press 1950.

20. W. H. Thorpe, *Science, Man and Morals*, Methuen 1965.

21. Simpson, op. cit., p.260: 'man's associated perceptual, co-ordinating and reacting apparatus is incomparably the best ever evolved.'

22. Ibid., p.262.

23. M. Polanyi, *The Tacit Dimension*, Routledge and Kegan Paul 1967, p.47.

24. It is because the biological evolution of man has now been superseded by this psycho-social development, which involves an interplay of the Darwinian combination of heredity, environment and mutation with man's conscious choice of what he makes of his environment, and what he makes of himself, that one can only see the next stage of development as some kind of inner transformation of man himself – of his values and his ability to attain their true expression. But this is precisely what the Christian gospel is, namely, that in and through Christ men have the opportunity of attaining their true ends, those for which God made them, and of experiencing that inner transformation which constitutes the essence of 'eternal life' in the Holy Spirit of God. In Christ, God the Word was made *our* flesh (John 1.14), the Word to us as men, whatever form his Word may be to other intelligent beings who may exist now or in the future in the universe.

25. The approach outlined in this chapter has been adumbrated long since in William Temple's *Nature, Man and God*, Macmillan 1934, ch.XIX. But there he writes in somewhat Hegelian terms, and it is hoped that the approach offered here provides a contemporary elaboration of Temple's penetrating insight into the relevance of the Christian sacraments for providing the basis of a unified view of matter and of 'spirit'. The approach is also similar to that presented in L. S. Thornton, *The Incarnate Lord*, Longmans 1928.

26. C. E. Raven, *Natural Religion and Christian Theology*, Gifford Lectures, Cambridge University Press 1953, vol.II, p.157.

27. Some might object that this view is too man-centred. Why should we suppose that man is the last stage of development? Briefly, this is taken to be the case because (1) scientifically speaking, man is now psycho-socially effective in his own evolution and in his effects on other species; and (2) theologically speaking, the 'Word was made flesh' of a *man*.

3

The 'Institution' Narratives and the Christian Eucharist

John Austin Baker

This paper is primarily concerned with a quite limited amount of New Testament material: the four accounts (in Mark, Matthew, Luke, and I Corinthians) of the so-called 'institution' of the eucharist. Though a good deal of further evidence of one sort and another will come into the discussion, these will be the focus of attention. What are their background, form, and setting? What in them do we owe to Jesus himself, and what to the church? And, above all, how are we to understand their relation to the eucharist? It is at this last point in particular that thoughts suggest themselves which may be pertinent to our present-day liturgical concerns: but this final question can hardly be usefully discussed, if the problems inherent in the two previous ones have not been at least clarified, and certain conventional assumptions challenged.

Sacrifice, Passover, and the Last Supper

There is no need to enter here into the long and technical debate, whether or not the Last Supper was a Passover meal. All we have to bear in mind is two points about which there is no dispute:

1. The Passion of Jesus occurred at Passover time. Passover associations were therefore inescapable: and these have left some mark on the interpretation of the Passion in the NT. Thus, Paul in I Cor. 5.7 writes: 'For our passover too was sacrificed, (namely) Christ'; and the Fourth Evangelist times the crucifixion to coincide with the slaying of the paschal lambs in the Temple precincts.[1] Finally, from a second century work, Justin's *Dialogue with Trypho* (72.1), we

have the well-known Jewish-Christian midrash, which must be much earlier, possibly even originating in NT times, since Justin honestly believes it to have been excised from the OT by the Jews: 'This passover is our saviour and our refuge ... we are to humble him on a cross (*sēmeion*) ...'

2. Mark, with Matthew and Luke following him, undoubtedly believed the Last Supper to have been the Passover meal. They may well have been correct historically; but whether they were or not, what matters for our present purposes is that their accounts are placed firmly in the context not merely of the Passover festival in general but of the actual paschal supper.[2]

A fashion has grown up in recent years of regarding this Passover setting as the vital key to a proper understanding of the Last Supper narratives in the NT.[3] It is held to explain not only the form of Jesus' symbolic action and the fact that he accompanied it with a verbal interpretation, but also the ideas which were in his mind at the time or, if we prefer, in the mind of the church when telling the story. For the former conviction there are solid grounds; for the latter, virtually none. It is rather more than time that the Passover factor was seen in its proper proportion.

In the first place, the really remarkable thing about the Passover motif in the NT is how *little* influence it has. Out of all the mass of material interpreting the death of Jesus in terms of OT types and predictions – the Suffering Servant, the Day of Atonement, the covenant-making on Sinai, the martyrdom of the prophets, and so on – only one verse (I Cor. 5.7) can be found which certainly and explicitly draws a parallel with the paschal sacrifice;[4] and even this verse drops this particular aspect immediately, and moves on to a moralizing exhortation based on imagery from the twin feast of Unleavened Bread.[5]

When we turn to the material of the institution narratives themselves, there are two distinct questions involved; and it is important to keep them clearly separated. The larger question is whether the material interprets Jesus' death as a sacrifice, and to this, the answer must be: 'Some of it does so, but not all' – and there is significance in which parts do and which do not. The smaller, more precise question is whether this sacrifice is paschal in character; and here, as we shall see, the answer, on a very decided balance, is 'No'. There will be no need at this stage to consider the inter-relation of the various accounts of the 'words', or problems of authenticity, and so forth, because all that concerns us at the moment is evidence of sacrificial or paschal connotations, wherever these may be found.

We begin with the basic elements in the material, the 'identification' of the bread with the body (flesh) and the cup with the blood. Jeremias argues[6] that the fact that there are two sayings, one referring to the flesh and the other to the blood, implies 'a slaying that has separated flesh and blood', and that this must allude to the ritual of sacrifice. It could, however, even more cogently be argued that Jesus was speaking of his flesh as food, since by the Law all animals have to be drained of blood before their meat can be eaten, and this would fit better the command, 'Take, eat'. But in fact neither 'food' nor 'sacrifice' interpretation is valid, since the parallel command to 'drink' the blood is quite incompatible with either model. Furthermore, the breaking of the loaf, though in the context of the words it is likely to be symbolism of some kind, can hardly be pressed to indicate anything more specific than death in general.

The same applies to the cup. Jeremias has two arguments here, neither of which will bear inspection. He regards the term 'poured out' (*ekkhunnomenon*) as 'from the language of sacrifice', remarking that '*ekkhein haima* is used in the LXX, apart from its use of murder or the domestic slaughter of cattle, only when speaking of sacrifice'.[7] Since there are not many other common situations of which such a phrase could be used, it would appear to be quite non-specific. Why then does it have to be the sacrificial usage here? Why not that of murder?[8] The second argument concerns the word 'blood'. He writes: '... a language usage which must be pre-Pauline because it is common in early Christianity ... sums up the saving power of the death of Jesus in the phrase "his blood". But the crucifixion itself was a bloodless form of execution. The phrase therefore does not come from a reminiscence of the form of execution but rather from the language of sacrifice, and it became generally accepted despite the fact that it did not correspond to what actually happened at Golgotha. The simplest explanation of this is that it was already a given fact to the earliest community', namely, in the words of Jesus at the Last Supper. Nevertheless, only two pages later[9] Jeremias refers in a different connection to a passage from Josephus (*Antt.* xix.94), which when cited in full points to exactly the opposite conclusion. The context is the performance in the theatre on the day of Caligula's assassination, and the relevant passage reads:

> In the first place a mime was presented in the course of which

The 'Institution' Narratives and the Christian Eucharist

a chieftain is caught and crucified. Moreover, the play presented by the dancer was *Cinyras*, in which the hero and his daughter Myrrha are killed. Thus a great quantity of artificial blood was shed, what with the crucified man and Cinyras.

Clearly Josephus did not regard crucifixion as a 'bloodless form of execution'.[10] The idea that the reference to blood must imply sacrificial blood is wholly without foundation.

When we come, however, to the concept of 'the blood of the covenant', which in various phrasings is included by Paul, Mark, and Matthew in their versions of the 'words of institution', the situation is very different. Here the thought is without doubt sacrificial; and the most obvious source is the OT Sinai tradition, specifically Ex. 24.8: 'And Moses took the blood and threw it upon the people, and said, "Behold the blood of the covenant which the Lord has made with you in accordance with all these words".' The Epistle to the Hebrews[11] treats this Sinai covenant-making in a way which is highly relevant to our present concerns. Sinai foreshadows the 'new' covenant, mediated by Jesus and made possible by his death; the fact that blood played a prominent part in the making of the first covenant is seen as, so to speak, explaining why the new covenant too had to be ratified with blood, in this case the blood of Jesus; and that blood-shedding was concerned, as this one is, with purification and the forgiveness of sins. In the course of this exposition the Epistle quotes the verse from Exodus given above, only in a form closer to the phrase familiar to us from one version of the institution narratives: 'This is the blood of the covenant which God commanded you' (*touto to haima tēs diathēkēs* ...).[12] We have, therefore, solid evidence to suggest what a phrase like 'blood of the covenant' could and did mean to at least one New Testament Christian when applied to the death of Jesus: a purificatory and expiatory sacrifice by means of which the new covenant foretold in the OT prophet was established between God and men. The type of this covenant-making was Sinai, the chief of only two occasions in the OT where the phrase in question occurs.[13]

There would not seem to be much connection here with the blood of the passover sacrifice. Jeremias, however, tries in two different ways to show that the passover blood could have been described as covenant-blood. The first is that the blood of the paschal lambs 'made operative' God's earlier covenant with Abraham. The authority here is Targ. Zech. 9.11;[14] but this is in no way to the point, since this Targum interprets the words of the prophet, 'the blood of thy covenant', as meaning the blood of the animals slain at the covenant-making in Gen. 15. This is not evidence for applying the phrase to the later paschal observance in Egypt. The second attempt is based on Mekilta Exodus 12.6, which quotes an exegesis of Ezek. 16.6-8 by Rabbi Matia ben Heresh (c. AD 125), concluding that the blood of the paschal sacrifice and the blood of circumcision were the two God-given duties which the Israelites had to perform in order to be worthy of redemption from Egypt. To this Zech. 9.11 is appended, as a further reference to the same subject.[15] This certainly looks more promising; but both Jeremias's interpretation of the rabbinic passage and its applicability are open to question. As regards the interpretation the difficulty briefly is this. In Ezek. 16.6 the word $b^e d\bar{a}m\bar{e}k$ ('in thy blood': MT: $b^e d\bar{a}mayik$) occurs twice;[16] the Midrash (Pirqe R. Eliezer XXIX) takes this as indicating that two different kinds of blood are meant, and fixes on the passover blood and the circumcision blood. R. Matia in his later and more elaborate exposition of the surrounding passage simply takes over this traditional exegesis of v.6 as it stands, adding the citation of Zech. 9.11. But the relevant quotation from R. Eliezer[17] makes it quite clear that the epithet 'covenant' attaches only to the circumcision blood. Hence it is virtually certain, given the scrupulousness of rabbinic exegesis, that the singular in Zech. 9.11 was taken by R. Matia also as referring to one only of his two 'bloods', namely that of circumcision; and in that event the description of passover blood as covenant blood is non-existent. But even if it could have been established, we would still have to ask whether it was properly applicable to our concern. Can we really use the collation of two OT texts by a rabbi of the early second century to interpret the mind of a Christian writer sixty years before (Mark), or of Jesus ninety years before?

Another element in the total tradition of the words is the reference to the shedding of blood 'for many' and 'for the forgiveness of sins'. Here, as with 'covenant', there can be no doubt that sacrificial ideas are in mind. Jesus' death is compared to the 'sin' or 'guilt' or 'atonement' offerings of Judaism. But again, what has this to do with Passover? Jeremias agrees that 'the passover of later times was not an expiatory but an ordinary sacrifice ... it could not be accepted as a substitute for the obligatory sin-offerings'.[18] But, he argues, this was not true of the first Passover, the one celebrated in Egypt under Moses; and he sets out to show that this was thought of in Judaism as expiatory, and thus that an expiatory interpretation by Jesus of his own death accords with his supposed vision of himself as the 'true paschal lamb', ushering in the perfect covenant and the full eschatological salvation. The two texts which he adduces, however, do not bear out his contention. The less important, Mekilta Exodus 12.13, implies no more than that the spreading of the paschal blood on the doorposts was a meritorious act of obedience which God rewarded by deliverance, and so does not involve expiatory ideas. The other, the one to which Jeremias attaches most weight, is the commentary in Exodus Rabba 15.12, which reads: 'It is as if a king said to his sons: Know you that I judge persons on capital charges and condemn them. Give me therefore a present, so that in case you are brought before my judgment seat I may set aside the indictments against you. So God said to Israel: I am now concerned with death penalties, but I will tell you how I will have pity on you and for the sake of the passover blood and the circumcision blood I will make atonement for your souls.'[19] If we compare the closing words of this passage with the similar OT formulas relating to atoning sacrifices, it is clear that the phrasing has been carefully chosen. Normally the subject of the verb k-p-r, 'to make atonement', is the human minister (cf. Ex. 29.36f.; 30.10,15,16; 32.30; Lev. 4.20,26,31,35; 5.6,10,13,16,18; 6.7 etc. etc.). In Lev. 17.11 God says of the blood: 'The life of the flesh is in the blood; and I have given it to you upon the altar to make atonement for your souls; for it is the blood that makes atonement, by reason of the life.' This passage is of special interest because it comes close in form to the final words of the comment quoted above from Exodus Rabba; but the very nearness draws attention to the difference. In Leviticus, too, God is the subject of the sentence; but he has done no more than give men the means whereby to make atonement if they choose. In Exodus Rabba God himself makes the atonement. The words, 'for the sake of the passover blood and the circumcision blood I will make atonement for your souls', show that the passover blood is not itself the means of atonement; for God assuredly does not need to use blood for this purpose.[20] The paschal offering, like the self-mutilation of circumcision, is a present or tribute which the Israelite pays to God, and in so doing distinguishes himself from the rest of mankind; and when one marked out in this way comes before God's judgment-seat, then God, instead of sentencing him to death, makes atonement for his life. This exegesis is faithful to the idea behind Ex. 12, where the blood of the lamb is a sign upon the houses of the

Israelites: '... and when I see the blood, I will pass over you, and no plague shall fall upon you to destroy you' (12.13). Passover here has certainly been drawn into the sphere of Later Judaism's developed atonement theology, but equally certainly not as itself an atonement.

The last remaining element in the words does not call for investigation here. Jeremias has proved beyond reasonable doubt that the phrase, 'Do this for my memorial (*anamnēsis*)' has its background in the Palestinian Judaism of the time of Jesus, and means, 'Do this that God may remember me, and bring in the kingdom for which I have given and am giving my life'. Jeremias has also made a very strong case for thinking that 'remembrance of the Messiah', in the sense of prayer for his coming, was part of the eschatological enthusiasm of the Passover festival at this period. Passover thus provides at any rate a plausible setting for this part of the tradition.

It also does so for the fact that Jesus chose to create the particular kind of gesture that he did, namely, the distribution and consumption of food and drink, and the giving of an explanatory commentary of this action. For this is the structure of the very heart of the Passover meal; the eating not only of the paschal lamb but also of certain symbolic dishes, and the giving of the Passover *haggada* by the head of the family. There is, of course, the radical difference that the paschal supper re-enacts and symbolically commemorates something that has already happened long ago, whereas Jesus in his symbolism is referring to something which has yet to occur. Nevertheless, there is clearly a generic similarity between the two sufficient to have given Jesus, so to speak, the idea for this corporate act by which his friends were to 'remember the Messiah' before God.

We see, therefore, taking the tradition as a whole, that its various elements fall into three categories: first, there are the general character of Jesus' action and the specific *anamnēsis* saying, both of which, though not referring to Jewish beliefs about the Passover, could have been suggested by it; secondly, there is the symbolic presentation of Jesus' death, without characterizing it in any particular way, namely, the breaking of the loaf accompanied by the words, 'This is my flesh', and the corresponding formula over the cup; and thirdly, there are the echoes of purificatory and expiatory sacrifice contained in such phrases as 'blood of the covenant', and 'for the forgiveness of sins', together with definite evocation of the first covenant-making on Sinai. The pattern that emerges here is suggestive: those elements that supply theological interpretation of the death of Jesus are non-paschal, even to some extent positively dissociated from the Passover; but what we may call the 'personal' elements – the creative conception and the form which it is given, the symbolizing of the fact of the death, the desire for vindication of one's cause by God in response to the prayer of friends – all this, though not specifically paschal, is at least natural and plausible in the setting which the NT gives it, the conjuncture of the paschal supper and the crisis of Jesus' life and calling on earth.

The Development and Authenticity of the Words

That Jesus must have said something unusual in connection with the bread and wine at the Last Supper may be taken for granted, especially if the loaf and cup in question were already part of the ritual of the paschal supper itself; for then there would have been nothing to attract attention to them unless he deliberately chose to do so. Moreover, the elements in the tradition which have the best claim to be considered original, or the starting-point of the whole development, are those which we have called the 'personal' ones, those that establish the fact that it is Jesus' death which is being symbolized. Interpretative words cannot just float about with nothing to interpret; and therefore, from the point of view of logical structure, if nothing else, the phrases referring to the covenant-blood, the forgiveness of sins, and so on, must be secondary to those defining the creative heart of the symbolic act. In short, the hard core of the words of institution is the phrases identifying the bread as Jesus' body and the cup as his blood. On this identification all the versions are agreed, except that in the shorter text of Luke the (first) cup is not identified with the blood. If we wish to be completely rigorous, therefore, and get down to bedrock, the ultimate reduction will be to the words, 'This is my body (flesh)' (Hebrew: *zeh b^{e}śarī*; Aramaic: *den(ā) bisrī*). Hebrew and Aramaic having no tenses in the temporal sense associated with European languages, the present of the verb 'to be' is not expressed. This raises no difficulty with regard to identity-statements, but it does inhibit the Judaism of the NT period from metaphysical pronouncements about 'existence' or 'being'. In the phrase under consideration, *zeh* or *den* points to the bread, and identifies it as 'my flesh' in the way appropriate to the context. That this way is not a literal equation of the bread with the biological flesh of Jesus, even a slight acquaintance with the mental temper of Judaism makes clear. Jesus could not have meant the words that way, and the disciples could not have taken them that way. The probability is, therefore, that the sign is a composite one. The eating is most naturally taken as a sign of fellowship; the words, 'This is my body', coupled with the breaking (which must have been an actual physical act, not just a manner of speaking, if the loaf was shared among the company), seem to refer to the coming death.

As is well known, this particular phrase is rendered in all four accounts of the words with the Greek term, *sōma*, 'body', for which there is no corresponding term in Hebrew or Aramaic. *gūph*, 'corpse', or, in post-biblical Hebrew, body as opposed to soul, is out of the question here. Jesus must have said, 'This is my *flesh*'; but why, then, was this not translated straightforwardly by *sarx*? That *sarx* could perfectly easily be used in a eucharistic context is shown by the Fourth Gospel.[21] One answer could be that all our four accounts are ultimately controlled by Paul's version. For Paul, *sarx* was ruled out by the special pejorative sense for which he largely reserves it in his theology,[22] while *sōma* offered attractive openings for theological exposition (cf. I Cor. 10.14-18). If Paul's choice of *sōma* for the Hebrew or Aramaic original became the normative rendering for teaching in and from his churches and by his friends, then we cannot rule this out as determining the usage of the Gospel of Mark, and through that Matthew, and also of Luke. If so, then we have here one possible clue to the inter-relation of the various accounts.

The parallel phrase, 'This is my blood', is involved with one notorious difficulty. There would have been no need to do more than allude to this in passing, had not the attempt recently been made to show that it does not really exist. Agreeable as this conclusion would be, however, it cannot be said yet to have been satisfactorily established. The problem in question is, of course, the fact that the words, 'This is my blood of the (new) covenant' (Mark, Matthew), cannot, as is generally supposed, be translated back into Hebrew or Aramaic. In Hebrew, for example *zeh dāmī bᵉrīt* is impossible; the suffix has to come at the end of the phrase, *zeh dam bᵉrītī*, of which the normal translation is, 'This is the blood of my covenant' (cf., e.g., Ps. 79.10: *dam ᵃbādeykā*, 'the blood of thy servants'). Jeremias, however, now believes that *zeh dam bᵉrītī* can be 'the Hebrew original of "my blood of the covenant" '.[23] His argument is as follows. In NT Greek we find phrases – e.g. Heb. 1.2: *ep'eskhatou tōn hēmerōn toutōn*, and 5.1: *hai hēmerai*

The 'Institution' Narratives and the Christian Eucharist 47

sarkos autou, where in meaning the closing pronominal genitive goes with the first noun in the composite phrase, not with the second. The sense of the two examples quoted is thus, 'in this end of the days', and 'his days of flesh'. Jeremias concludes: 'Correspondingly, we can presuppose as the Hebrew original of "my blood of the covenant" the expression *dam bᵉrītī*, Aramaic *'adam keyāmī* ("my covenant blood"), which in Greek could be rendered regularly and correctly only with the transposition of the personal pronoun.' There are a good many obscurities in this argument; but it does seem to be open to a number of fatal objections. The crux seems to be this: '...in Hebrew as well as in Aramaic, a construct state combination tolerates the suffix only at the end ... ; it is related then, however, to the whole expression'.[24]

The examples given to justify this assertion are the Greek phrases from Hebrews, quoted above. They are presumably regarded as semitisms (though this is not expressly stated), and thus as a guide to the meaning of the semitic phrase to which they literally correspond. In Hebrew, for example, *hai hēmerai tēs sarkos autou* would be *yᵉmē bᵉśārō*; and let us say at once that the latter phrase could perfectly well be rendered in English, 'his flesh days', as Jeremias desiderates. But the reason for this is nothing to do with syntax, but simply with the fact that there is no discernible difference in meaning between 'the days of his flesh' and 'his days of flesh'. We have only to apply the test to the words from Ps. 79.10, cited earlier, to see the point. If we make 'thy' in the phrase, 'the blood of thy servants', 'relate to the whole expression', we have, presumably, 'thy servant blood', which, when said of God, as here, is nonsense. How can we possibly decide the correct rendering, or the semantic potential, of a phrase or idiom in Hebrew or Aramaic on the basis of a supposed imitation in Greek? We must go to the evidence of the original language as decisive.

Jeremias' thesis is that the phrase with which we are primarily concerned – *touto esti to haima mou (to) tēs diathēkēs* (Mark 14.24; Matt. 26.28 – is a 'regular and correct' Greek way of rendering *dam bᵉrītī* (*'adam kevāmī*) in one possible meaning of the latter, namely, 'my covenant blood'. Is there, then, any solid *semitic* language evidence that this is a possible meaning? If, as in the case of *yᵉmē bᵉśārō*, there were no discernible difference of meaning between the two proposed renderings, that is, if 'the blood of my covenant' meant the same thing as 'my blood of the covenant', then of course there would be no problem. But it quite plainly does not. The former phrase, said over the cup, would hardly have given rise to centuries of frenzied strife and debate. The blood has to be 'my blood', as the body is 'my body'; and a moment's reflection will show that the blood in the phrase *dam bᵉrītī* very certainly does not have to be the blood of the speaker, any more than the *dam bᵉrītēḵ* of Zech. 9.11 has to be the blood of Israel. If Jesus indeed said *zeh dam bᵉrītī*, then, in the light of everything we know about Hebrew, there was no reason whatever for anyone to suppose that he was referring to his own death.

Jeremias, however, wishes to back both the horses in a two-horse race, and therefore includes a note on the possibility that the Markan and Matthaean phrase does represent the order of words in a semitic original.[25] Can a pronominal suffix perhaps tolerate a genitive after itself? In fact, however, the parallels suggested by various scholars are not really adequate. The best, as Jeremias points out, is Dan. 2.34,[26] '... and it smote the image on *its feet of iron and clay*'. But Aramaic has here a flexibility which Hebrew lacks, in its ability to indicate the genitive by *di*; and the relation here is the specific one of the material out of which something is made. It would be precarious, therefore, to extend it to an Aramaic original of the words of institution, and impossible if these were in Hebrew. Another possible parallel, not so far noted, comes in Ps. 45.6, where the phrase *kissᵉḵā 'ᵉlōhīm* is rendered by some modern versions 'thy divine throne' (or, if we assume the superlative use of *'ᵉlōhīm*, 'thy supreme throne'). Unfortunately, however, the only objection to rendering straightforwardly, 'Thy throne, O divine one!', is the feeling or hope of pious commentators that no Israelite would ever say such a thing of a human ruler. We cannot, therefore, be sure that this is a true parallel.

The case, then, for regarding the words 'of the covenant' appended to 'This is my blood' as 'an old theological interpretation which ... designates Jesus' expiatory death as a covenant sacrifice for the inauguration of the final salvation'[27] still stands. But the linguistic objection cannot be raised against the form of the cup-saying in Paul: 'This cup is the new covenant in my blood.' Why, then, could we not take this as the original form, especially as it occurs in a piece of tradition widely accepted as deriving from the primitive Jerusalem community itself? If, however, we are thinking not just of a very early tradition, but of an authentic recollection of the Last Supper, this Pauline form is unlikely to be correct. The main reason for rejecting it is that the element in the total phrase which goes

The 'Institution' Narratives and the Christian Eucharist 49

naturally with 'covenant' is not 'cup' but 'blood'. The phrase, 'This cup (i.e. its contents) is my blood of the (new) covenant', however unexpected or shocking, is a sequence of terms which can be followed; 'This cup is the new covenant in my blood' is back-handed and awkward. Since Jesus is portrayed as using straightforward and very clear parallelism on other occasions also, the weight of probability must be on the side of a basic 'This is my body – This is my blood' structure.

But if so, how then are we to explain the fact that the earliest account reads as it does? The inference to be drawn, surely, is that the interpretation of the blood as covenant-blood is a theological construction of the very earliest community. Jesus, making the statement for the first time, would hardly use the wrong-way-round arrangement, 'This is the covenant in my blood'; Jewish Christians who understood the blood of Calvary as a new covenant-making could, however, put it this way, because they already knew that the cup was the blood, and they had to put it this way, because their language would not allow them to do it differently. The Markan version, composed in Greek, made the two sayings parallel once more, not consciously returning to a more original historical tradition – the presence of the covenant element rules that out – but in the interests of a neat parallelism which Greek could perfectly well manage. This points, therefore, to the following sequence:

Jesus:	This (cup) is my blood
Jerusalem and Paul:	This (cup) is the new covenant in my blood
Mark and Matthew:	This is my blood of the covenant.

Such a sequence is both possible in itself, and also accounts for the main features in our material. We may therefore take it as a reasonable conjectural reconstruction, if no more, of what the original words of Jesus may have been at this point.

We turn next to another element in the tradition of the words, that of the commands. A resumé of the data may be helpful.

1. In I Cor. 11.23ff. there are two commands: 'Do this in remembrance of me', at the distribution of the bread; and, 'Do this, as often as you drink it, in remembrance of me', at the giving of the cup.
2. In Mark 14.22ff. Jesus says over the bread, 'Take; this is my

body'. At the cup no command is expressed, but it is stated that 'they all drank of it'.

3. In Matt. 26.26ff. the words over the bread are, 'Take, eat; this is my body'; and over the cup, 'Drink of it all of you, for this is my blood', etc.

4. In Luke 22.14ff. (shorter version) Jesus' words when giving the cup are, 'Take this and divide it among yourselves'; at the bread simply, 'This is my body'. (The longer version introduces the Pauline 'Do this in remembrance of me' after the bread.)

An element of command is present, therefore, in all the accounts; but there are important differences, which we must examine.

The words 'as often as you drink it' are peculiar to I Corinthians. They are significant as being the only words in all the material which indicate quite unambiguously that this is an action to be repeated on later occasions, and not just a once for all gesture. The rite is in fact to continue until the Second Coming. The *anamnēsis*, as we saw, is a remembering of Jesus before God in order to hasten the coming of the kingdom; and after the resurrection of Jesus the bringing in of the kingdom meant for Christians the return of their Lord. Thus we arrive at Paul's closing comment on the Last Supper tradition: 'For as often as you eat this bread and drink this cup, you proclaim the Lord's death until he comes' (I Cor. 11.26), and at the prayer, *Marana tha*, 'Our Lord, come!', attested by Paul (I Cor. 16.22), and placed by the *Didache* (10.6) in a eucharistic setting.

In considering this Pauline version of the Last Supper command it is important to be clear what it is the disciples are commanded to do. Certainly not what we might naturally answer, namely, repeat the words of Jesus over the bread and wine. 'This is my body ... Do this' cannot on any normal use of language mean 'Repeat the words, "This is my body etc."'. The natural reference in Paul's account is to what Jesus himself has just done: take bread, give thanks,[28] break. (The mention of 'eating' in 11.26 makes explicit what is already implicit in the breaking.) Christians are to take bread and wine, give thanks over them ('likewise also the cup': v. 25), and eat and drink, all as a memorial prayer.

We see now the main similarity and the main difference between Paul's version and that of the Synoptists. In Mark and Matthew the command, explicit or implicit, is again to 'take', or 'take and eat', the bread, and to 'drink' the cup; in Luke, to 'share' the cup. That is the element in common: the command to eat and drink. The differences are: first, that in the Synoptists there is no command to

The 'Institution' Narratives and the Christian Eucharist 51

'give thanks'; secondly, that the action is not described as a 'memorial', indeed, it is not described as anything; thirdly, that there is no indication that the action is to be repeated – in fact, if the Synoptists were the only source of information we had, there would be nothing to show that the command element was not a once for all, *ad hoc* command solely to those present on this unique occasion. In short, *in the Synoptists anything which might make the story into a liturgical directive for the church is missing*. We, naturally enough, cannot help reading the passages in question as though they are a model for the eucharist; but this does not alter the fact that the writers have done nothing to make it clear whether this is so – a failure which the longer version of Luke is presumably meant to repair.

Now, it can legitimately be argued that, since the 'breaking of bread' was an integral part of Christian life from the first, it would no more have been possible for the evangelist to write or his congregation to read or hear this story without thinking of it in eucharistic terms than it is for us. Considerable support for such a view has been provided by a recent study which shows how pervasive the influence of eucharistic thinking is throughout Mark's gospel.[29] This means, therefore, that in comparing the two basic forms of the tradition, the Pauline and the Synoptic, we have to ask ourselves why the one is explicitly liturgically oriented whereas the other, on the surface at any rate, is apparently more concerned with the narrative of a once for all event and with using that narrative to express the theological significance of the death of Jesus. There are various possible answers, not necessarily mutually exclusive. The difference could result, for instance, from the fact that the Synoptic account is fairly rigorously disciplined by its Passion narrative setting, whereas Paul's version of the tradition was designed for missionary catechesis (I Cor. 11.23: 'I received from the Lord what I also delivered to you'), and so with explaining Christian religious practice. Or again, it could be that readers who knew that the Last Supper was the source of the eucharist did not need to have this spelled out for them – the point made by Benoit in his celebrated aphorism on the absence of the 'Do this' clause from Mark: 'On ne récite pas une rubrique, on l'exécute.' Paul's version, in other words, was the one for catechumens; the gospels are for the instructed, practising Christian.

Two final points remain for this section of our enquiry. First, it is important to remember that for the two major elements of theological interpretation in the words of institution, those relating to 'covenant' and 'atonement' sacrifice, no foundation has been laid in any other of the recorded words of Jesus. Nowhere is he shown as referring in any context to the covenant concept or the OT covenant events; if it were not for the Last Supper narrative, we would almost certainly conclude that this was an element in Judaism which he ignored or even rejected. But the Matthaean phrase about 'the forgiveness of sins' exhibits an even greater discrepancy, a positive contrast to the rest of Jesus' teaching. Jesus deals constantly with the question of the forgiveness of sins; and he does so in unvarying terms. God will forgive the sins of anyone who asks for forgiveness, and who forgives the sins of others against himself. Christians pray this every day of their lives; and Jesus clearly sees it as a permanent fact of the God-man relationship. Why, then, should he suddenly present his own death as the means whereby forgiveness is to be made available? That his death is regarded as such a means in various parts of the NT is indisputable; but we must ask whether this is not precisely one of those interesting items on which Jesus appears to be at variance with the church.

The second point is this. Between the Last Supper and the church stands the transforming fact of the resurrection. We have seen that Paul's comment on the institution tradition acknowledges this; the death is 'remembered' only until and in expectation of the return. In the Gospel accounts the resurrection is also present, but not in the central phrases which we have been considering. It is implicit in the words: 'Truly, I say to you, I shall not drink again of the fruit of the vine until that day when I drink it new in the kingdom of God' (Mark 14.25; cf. Matt. 26.29; Luke 22.15,18). Whether we consider these words historical or simply dramatically appropriate makes no difference at this point; reference to the resurrection in this context was bound to be prophetic in form.

That the resurrection of Jesus was an essential constituent of the eucharistic thinking of the NT is clear from such well-known instances as the Emmaus story (Luke 24.13-35), John 21, and the words attributed to Peter in Acts 10.41. But we have to face the fact that those elements in the NT accounts which came to form the hard core of liturgical observance were the ones which interpreted, and related solely to the death of Christ, to the exclusion of his resurrection. To the question of liturgical use we must now very briefly turn.

Liturgical Formula or 'Hieros Logos'?

It is an accepted starting-point of much modern discussion of the eucharist that the NT words of institution are liturgical. This assumption, however, may at least be reasonably questioned. For while it is well known that from an early date the words of institution figure in the eucharistic rite, the evidence for the earliest period of all is not by any means as strong as it is claimed to be, and is in fact susceptible of a different interpretation.

When Jeremias tries to go back behind the *Apostolic Tradition* of Hippolytus, the available evidence is confined to two sources – the *Didache* and Justin Martyr's *First Apology*. As regards the *Didache* he takes the position of Zahn and Dibelius that *Did.* 9.1-10.5 gives us the prayers of the *agape* before and after the meal, 10.6 the introductory liturgy to the following eucharist.[30] 'The Eucharist itself is not described'.[31] It is, of course, possible to take a different view, and to ask in what way something which is called *eucharistia* (*Did.* 9.1), in which thanks are given over a cup and over broken bread (9.2,3), in which only the baptized can partake (9.5), and which is called 'holy' (*hagios*), something not to be given to 'dogs', that is, outsiders (9.5, quoting Matt. 7.6), is essentially different from what we mean by a eucharist. In the opinion of the present writer, in no essential way whatever. The proceedings described in the *Didache*, especially when we remember their strongly eschatological note (10.5,6), seem (except for the inverted order of the cup and the bread) to be a very adequate following out of the instructions contained in the pre-Pauline tradition of I Cor. 11.23ff. But on the other view, of course, it is necessary to assume that the eucharistic liturgy proper is not described at all; and then a reason has to be found for this reticence.

The answer proposed is a desire 'to protect the sacred formula'. (The argumentation is decidedly circular, since we have yet to prove that there was a 'sacred formula' to protect.) This is a motive which scholars are rather apt to see popping up all over the place, often where it is invisible to the ordinary spectator. Thus, with regard to Luke-Acts, Jeremias writes: 'In the gospel, following his source, Luke quotes the eucharistic words; but in Acts, speaking for himself, he refers to the Lord's Supper exclusively in allusions and ambiguous phrases: "the breaking of bread" (2.42), "to break bread" (2.46; 20.7,11), perhaps also "food" (2.46) and "to taste" (20.11).' The last two examples are found only in conjunction with the phrase 'to break bread', and so have little relevance in this context. As for the rest, the argument is not strong. How are we to know whether the phrase 'the breaking of bread' or 'to break bread', which to an outsider would mean simply 'to take a meal', was in fact an esoteric Christian *terminus technicus* for the sacred rite, and not just plain description of it? Can we be so sure that Luke is 'speaking for himself' in Acts, and not using earlier material? Above all, why, if so anxious to protect the sacred formula, did he not omit or obscure it in the gospel, which purports to be addressed to the same reader, real or fictitious, as Acts? Jeremias believes that Luke did in fact do just this, quoting only the opening words of the 'sacred formula'. But the opening words, in this case 'This is my body', are surely the nub of the whole matter; the rest is commentary. Jeremias also refers to Pliny's Letter to Trajan, commenting: '... the slander that Christians held Thyestean meals ... was a consequence of the esoteric character of the eucharistic celebrations'.[32] But not solely of their 'esoteric character' – the slander must arise from a misconstruction of the statement that the bread and wine are the body and blood of a human being. Unless, as is certainly possible, we assume misrepresentation by ex-Christians with a grievance, this is not very good evidence for a rigid *disciplina arcani*.

Justin, in a famous passage (*I Apol.* 66.3ff.), shows that in his day the words of institution had become part of the thanksgiving over the bread and wine. He has no reluctance to quote them for pagan readers, because he is vitally concerned to convince them that what is consumed is not human flesh and blood, and the best way to do that is to make it clear how the notion could have arisen, by quoting the words and explaining the background of the rite without disguise.

The theory of the *disciplina arcani* does not, in fact, accommodate the evidence from the early period very convincingly; but then, of course, there is really no need to resort to it at all. A much simpler explanation will cover the facts, namely, that the words of institution were not, in NT times and immediately after, a sacred formula, and were not a necessary part of the eucharistic prayer. This would explain their absence from the *Didache*, and also, perhaps more significantly, the great variety of forms in which they occur in the NT itself. There is certainly no evidence there of liturgical stereotyping; on the contrary, the freedom with which they are expanded and moved around is much more typical of the ordinary gospel material.

If we bear this in mind, it may also throw a new light on the earliest account of the words, namely that of Paul. This passage raises one question so obvious that it is surprising how often it is overlooked: if these words were indeed the regular liturgical formula, why does Paul have to remind the Corinthians of the fact that he had passed on to them this particular piece of teaching? Paul does not speak as though he were reawakening them to something to which constant use had made them indifferent. He recalls a basic point in their early catechesis and stresses that he had not omitted it. When, too, we recall what was said earlier – first, that the command to 'do this' cannot mean that we are to repeat the words 'This is my body' or 'This is my blood'; and secondly, that in the Synoptists anything which might make the story into a liturgical directive for the church is missing – then the interpretation of the earliest evidence just advanced is certainly strengthened, and we find ourselves seriously asking whether in the NT there is any liturgical formula in the words of institution at all, or only a *hieros logos*, a sacred story giving the background and reason of the rite.

Why, then, and how do we arrive at the later position, in which Jesus' brief but pregnant interpretation of his symbolic gesture becomes the indispensable, almost magical heart of the eucharistic prayer? To answer such a question is clearly beyond the scope of this paper, concerned as it must be only with the NT period and that immediately succeeding. But it is of the utmost importance to appreciate that it is a question the NT poses, and which cannot be answered from within the NT itself. Among many possible factors are the early designation of the eucharist as the Christian 'sacrifice', under the influence of Mal. 1.11 (cf. *Did.* 14.3), and the fading of eschatological enthusiasm, which led to a view of the eucharist not as prayer for salvation but as actual experience of it, the 'medicine of immortality', with an inevitable injection of new significance into the words 'This *is* my body'. There is also undoubtedly an unbalanced concentration on the cross and death of Christ, especially in the interpretation suggested by the gospel versions of the words of institution, that of the atoning sacrifice; but this is something which gains ground most noticeably only after the spirit and atmosphere of the NT age has passed away, and when the witness of that age is present only in the petrified form of normative literary remains. It is perhaps not too much to say that it is precisely because the institution narratives were later regarded as liturgical directives that the church's life and witness have been disfigured by the long misery of eucharistic dissension.

Concluding Undogmatic Postscript

Many factors other than the evidence of the NT must control our eucharistic thinking and liturgical decisions; nor is it easy to say exactly how the ideas prompted by NT study are to be brought to bear on such practical contemporary matters. In these concluding remarks, therefore, the emphasis will be on the freedoms which the NT seems to legitimate for us rather than on any necessarily dubious prescriptions.

First, we are offered a very large freedom in the content and construction of our eucharistic prayers. We are not obliged to use the institution narrative or the words; and if we do, they supply us only with a narrative reminder of the reason why our central act of worship takes the form it does, the action around and over bread and wine. These physical data are the only things to which we are tied, the medium of our *anamnēsis*. What we say should be composed of the faith by which we live, as we see it, and as we wish to express it, bringing out of our treasures things new and old.

Secondly, we are released into a wholeness of faith, because we are free to structure our eucharist in terms of where we are, on this side of the resurrection. Misusing the story of the Last Supper constantly drags us back into a dramatic time which is not our real time; consequently the resurrection is tagged on as an afterthought – 'remembering also his resurrection from the dead, his glorious ascension....' The eucharist is not a re-enactment of the Last Supper; it is a fellowship meal with the risen Christ in whom we are one with the Father and have God the Spirit indwelling in our hearts, at which we look *back* with gratitude to the sacrifice which made this blessedness possible, and which gives us assurance of the greater blessedness to come. Only because of the resurrection are we in this situation; and so a eucharist which does not have post-resurrection existence as its axis is not a proper eucharist at all.

Thirdly and lastly, it would seem that in the institution Jesus himself, inspired though he may have been at the level of creative imagination by the great festival in which he and his friends were taking part, did not tie himself down nor seek to tie them to any particular Old Testament interpretation of what he was doing – and *a fortiori* he did not tie us. We are not obliged to use (or fraudulently misuse) tags such as 'the sacrifice of praise and thanksgiving', much less to endure the iron restriction of 'a full, perfect, and sufficient sacrifice, oblation, and satisfaction for the sins of the whole world'. We have good reason to believe that the interpretation which this represents was applied to the rite not by him but by one school of thought among his followers; and that he himself simply implied that his body and blood were 'for us'. It is ours to decide in his Spirit what that 'for us' involves, only so as it is him on whom we 'feed in our hearts by faith with thanksgiving'.

NOTES

1. In John 19.36 an OT 'prediction', 'Not a bone of him shall be broken', is said to have been fulfilled in the crucifixion. This in all probability is another paschal allusion, viz., to Ex. 12.46 or Num. 9.12; but it is just possible that the reference is to God's care for the righteous man in Ps. 34.20.

2. Paul's account of the Last Supper (I Cor. 11.23-5) is compatible with a passover meal (*n.b.* esp. v.25: 'In the same way also the cup, after supper ...'), but does not demand it, and certainly does not mention it.

3. The classic modern exposition of this approach is the great work by J. Jeremias, *Die Abendmahlsworte Jesu* (ET, *The Eucharistic Words of Jesus*, SCM Press ²1966, to which references are made: =*EWJ*). This presentation will, therefore, be discussed here. Dissent on detailed points does not imply anything less than admiration for this monumental study.

4. Jeremias, *EWJ* pp.82, 223n.1, counts I Peter 1.19; Rev. 5.6,9,12; 12.11; and John 1.29,36 all as references to the passover lamb. In the case of Revelation the imagery makes this wildly improbable. In John 1.29,36 the reference can be to the paschal lamb only if that lamb was thought of as an atonement sacrifice; and this, as we shall see, is precisely the point in dispute. I Peter 1.19 is the strongest case, especially if the theory that I Peter contains a 'paschal homily' is accepted; but there are strong objections to his theory, and though the reference is clearly to a sacrificial lamb of some kind, the stipulation that the victim should be 'without blemish' is applied in the OT not only to the paschal lamb (Ex. 12.5) but also to lambs offered on the altar (cf. Lev. 1.10; 23.12; Num. 6.12,14). The verse must remain a possible but not proven extra example.

5. Cf. Luke's (inaccurate) opening to the Passion narrative: 'Now the feast of Unleavened Bread drew near, which is called the Passover' (22.1). On the significance for our subject of the Passover in John, cf. the essay by C. F. Evans, pp.59ff. below.

6. *EWJ*, pp.221f.

7. *EWJ*, p.222, incl. n.5.

8. Jeremias himself agrees that the use of the word shows that 'Jesus did expect a violent death' (p.225).

9. *EWJ*, p.225n.1.

10. Trans. by L. H. Feldman (*Josephus*, vol.IX, Loeb edition, pp.258-61). The Fourth Evangelist does, of course, say that Jesus' blood was shed (19.34), though by a different means. In any case, Jesus might have expected that his blood would be shed, even if he had later turned out to be mistaken.

11. Heb. 8.1-9.22, esp. 9.15-22.

12. Heb. 9.20.

13. The other is Zech. 9.11, where the reference is either to Sinai (so most modern commentators) or to the covenant with Abraham (the Targum, some ancient Jewish commentators and a minority of moderns).

14. Cf. n.13 above.

15. The relevant passage is quoted in full, *EWJ*, p.225 n.5.

16. It is probably this double occurrence, and not the belief that the word should be read as a dual, as Jeremias suggests, which is responsible for the exegesis in the Midrash.

17. Also given by Jeremias, *EWJ*, p.225 n.4.

18. *EWJ*, p.225.

19. *EWJ*, p.226 n.2.

20. Not, *pace* the writer of Hebrews, to the Jewish mind, anyhow!

21. John 6 *passim*. For a discussion of the issues of this complex chapter see C. F. Evans, pp.62ff. below.

22. In John, of course, it is *kosmos* which plays something like the rôle of *sarx* in Paul, while *sarx* is free from any derogatory note (cf. 'the word became *sarx*': 1.14).

23. *EWJ*, p.195; for Jeremias' argument in full cf. pp.193ff.

24. *EWJ*, p.194.

25. *EWJ*, p.193 n.2.

26. Suggested by H. F. D. Sparks: cf. *EWJ*, p.193 n.2.

27. *EWJ*, p.194.

28. The giving of thanks cannot include the words, because Jesus' thanksgiving was already complete when he said them ('when he had given thanks, he broke it, and said ...').

29. Q. Quesnell, *The Mind of Mark*, Analecta Biblica 38, Rome 1969.

30. *EWJ*, p.118.

31. *EWJ*, p.134.

32. *EWJ*, p.135.

4

The Eucharist and Symbolism in the New Testament

C. F. Evans

The actions and words of the Last Supper are set by the synoptic evangelists deliberately and emphatically in the context of the Passover (Mark 14.12-26; Matt. 26.17-30; Luke 22.7-19). Nevertheless they are illuminated by this context only to a limited extent. This is so even if the details of the account – reclining at table, the use of wine, 'memorial' etc. – are rightly held to indicate a Passover context. For the oddity remains of a Passover meal without reference to the central feature of the lamb, and a connection between the actions and words of the Last Supper and the lamb is not readily made. The very fact that more than one reconstruction of the scene has been possible, and even that no very precise picture emerges of what was being done and intended, shows that the Passover context had not been so indelibly stamped on these actions and words in the tradition as to provide the sole and obvious clue to their meaning. The only other instance of the tradition in the New Testament, that in I Cor. 11.23-5, reveals it as having been received and handed on by Paul apart from a Passover context and with a setting provided by the words 'In the same night that he was handed over'.

What brought about this state of affairs would appear to have been both the brevity, compared with any Passover *haggadah*, of the interpretative words accompanying the twin actions at the Supper, as these were handed down in the tradition, and also their strong christological concentration. Whatever the precise interpretation to be given to these words – whether body-blood is a word pair already denoting a sacrificial victim (so Jeremias), or body is to be taken on its own, perhaps in the sense of 'self', and blood on its own in the sense of 'death' – the accent falls on Christ's person and passion. These characteristics may have caused or allowed the narrative of the Last Supper to become unhinged from any Passover context which it may once have had in the tradition, and to which the synoptic evangelists attempt, not wholly successfully, to tie it back. The actions and words as it were rode free, and were open to interpretation in terms of whatever Christ, his person and passion, were held to be.

This may be seen in St Paul's use of the tradition. The wider context of his warnings on the dangers of idolatry in I Cor. 10 may be called in a general sense a Passover context, since he makes reference to the crossing of the sea, to Moses, to the manna and the rock, and to the experiences of the Israelites in the desert (I Cor.10.1-13). But even here it is the food and drink in the desert that he fastens on, and he understands them as 'spiritual' (heavenly, supernatural, symbolic?), the latter expressly by reason of its source in Christ as the Rock. In the particular application in I Cor. 10.14-22 he expounds the eucharistic actions of eating and drinking (now in reverse order) in terms of a participation in Christ, in his death and in his body ('person'?), from which the conclusion is drawn that the many are a unity in Christ. In the following chapter, where he rehearses the tradition itself, he invites the Corinthians to judge whether their behaviour is consonant with communion in a meal which could be called 'the Lord's Supper'. This phrase is remarkable, since the adjective *kuriakos* ('of the Lord') is wanting in the LXX, and is found again in the New Testament only at Rev. 1.10, though it is frequent in inscriptions with reference to the emperor. Whether the phrase is a title for the meal or an adjectival description of what it should be, it attaches the significance of the meal – whether Last Supper, Christian Passover, or whatever – to what the Lord is. So also the eschatological framework of the meal, which is secured in the synoptists by the expectation of drinking wine new in the kingdom of God (in Luke of the fulfilment of the Passover itself in the kingdom of God), now becomes the proclamation of the Lord's death until he comes (I Cor. 11.17-26). This would suggest that if 'symbolism' has to be introduced into eucharistic theology, this is not because of the original character of the meal. Indeed, the Passover was the least symbolic of Jewish observances, since it involved the repetition of actual features in the original event – the lamb, the unleavened bread, the bitter herbs – upon which the *haggadah* was a commentary. It will rather be because

The Eucharist and Symbolism in the New Testament 61

of the 'symbolic' element inherent in the christology, the statement of who the Lord is.

This becomes evident in the only other explicit treatment of the matter in the New Testament, that in the Fourth Gospel. Here, as elsewhere, this evangelist's free handling of the tradition both poses acute questions concerning the location of this gospel within early Christianity, and also serves to concentrate the theological issues on the person of Christ. This gospel also has a meal 'on the night that he was given up', but it lacks any actions and words over bread and wine. After an initial cleansing of the disciples the time is devoted to a long prophetic and didactic discourse of the Lord issuing in his prayer, in which he declares the significance of his person and work in relation to the will of the Father, the disciples and the world. How far this discourse and prayer themselves rest upon a background of eucharistic practice and contain eucharistic undertones is a matter of debate. What is generally agreed is that the sixth chapter of this gospel is some kind of equivalent of the synoptic account of the Last Supper. Here also the Passover provides the context, and there is reference to the manna and to Moses. This, however, is marginal. It is Passover time in Galilee and not the actual celebration of the Passover in Jerusalem, and while there is a great deal in the Passover ritual of blessing God for the gifts of food and drink, the manna does not figure in it, except once in a list of the benefits conferred by God on Israel stretching from the deliverance from Egypt to entry into the promised land. The discourse proceeds, rather, out of the feeding of the five thousand, that is, from one of those actions which are consistently called '*sēmeia*' in this gospel and which can characterize the whole ministry of the Lord (John 2.11; 12.37; 20.30f.) as also his death (John 12.33; 18.31-2). Whereas 'symbol' would not be a completely adequate rendering for '*sēmeion*', since it need not preserve either the importance of the physical event itself or the reference forward to what the actions of Jesus promise for the future, nevertheless the symbolic is an indispensable element of what is meant here by a 'sign'. For the antithesis in this gospel is not so much between the present and the future as between the visible and the invisible, the exterior and the interior, and the sign is a pointer to the invisible reality as embodied in Christ. The purpose of a discourse is often to clarify this, and in doing so it sometimes makes use of the 'I am' formula to identify Christ with this reality. This is further stressed if it is correct (with Bultmann) to see the 'I am' formula when used in this way not as a presentation formula ('I am the one who...'), nor as an identification formula ('I am X...'), but as a recognition formula in which the 'I' is not the subject but the predicate – 'the living bread it is I'. For then the Johannine discourses would be resting on a background of thought in which certain symbolic expressions were already current as descriptive of divine, heavenly entities or concepts – *the* (true, i.e. heavenly) bread or vine, *the* living water, *the* light of the world, *the* resurrection, *the* way, *the* truth and *the* life. Christ is to be recognized as the embodiment of these. Or, one might perhaps say, men have certain basic needs as men; they are in search of nourishment, understanding, creative satisfaction, and of full and authentic life. For these needs to be formulated adequately to men as creatures of the divine Creator and as sons of the divine Father symbolic expressions have to be used, and Christ has to be spoken of with reference to them. Much of the christology of the Fourth Gospel is conveyed in this way. Because Christ is of the kind he is, language has to be used which is non-literal but which at the same time does not leave the literal entirely behind.

The discourse in John 6 is of particular importance in respect of some of these issues. As a discourse it is complicated in two ways. First, since it proceeds from a miracle of loaves, and treats of the living bread of which the perishable manna is a type, statements about blood and the drinking of blood (6.53-6) are bound to strike as forced and intrusive. They could hardly be there unless the thought of the satisfaction of men by the true and heavenly bread was being related to eucharistic practice in the church with its origins in the Last Supper. Secondly, there is a strange alternation between the strongest possible emphasis on the necessity for eternal life of eating the flesh and drinking the blood of the Son of Man (6.53-8) and the statement in 6.63 which appears to contradict and negate it: 'It is the Spirit which gives life; the flesh is good for nothing. The words that I have spoken to you are Spirit and are life.' Moreover, the issues raised in this discourse are regarded as so crucial that not only do they arouse the bitter hostility of the Jews with the crude charge of cannibalism (6.52), but they also bring about a large-scale defection of disciples at this point (6.60-67 – with this may perhaps be compared the statements in I John 2.18-26; 4.1-6 that many supposed prophets and spiritual people had left the Christian community, apparently through offence at the 'flesh' of Christ).

It is hardly surprising if commentators have found themselves

The Eucharist and Symbolism in the New Testament 63

somewhat baffled by this chapter, and especially by the questions whether it is properly called 'eucharistic', and if so in what sense. In the Detached Note, 'The Interpretation of the Sixth Chapter', which Hoskyns felt it necessary to append to his commentary at this point, he reflected on this[1]. He noted three main lines of interpretation. (*a*) The language is metaphorical throughout, and v.63 makes this clear. What is eaten and drunk is the Lord's words, and if the evangelist had the eucharist in mind at all he has completely spiritualized it. Some of the Reformers followed this line when they applied the eating and drinking to the assimilation by faith of the benefits of Christ's sacrifice. (*b*) The language of vv.51-8 is sacramental, but it is in contradiction not only with v.63 but with the rest of the discourse. These verses are therefore a later addition and are to be put down to ecclesiastical redaction (so now, Bultmann; though presumably at some stage the text in its present form would have to be interpreted). (*c*) The discourse is homogeneous and is sacrificial and sacramental throughout, but this is because in it the Christian religion has been assimilated to non-Jewish cults, and v.63 means the consecration of the eucharistic elements to be the food of immortality. Hoskyns himself dissents from all these views because he sees the situation of the evangelist as that of one who is faced on the one hand by a misunderstanding of the gospel of the flesh or historical existence of Christ as crude materialism, and on the other hand by an anti-sacramental movement of pure Spirit within Christianity. For this reason he regards patristic exegesis of the chapter as on the whole more satisfactory than the modern, because the Fathers tended not to refer its language exclusively either to feeding on the words of Jesus or to the sacrament. If by the eucharist is meant a rite once instituted and operating autonomously with its meaning and efficacy in itself, then this discourse is not 'about' the eucharist and should not be called 'eucharistic'. If, however, the eucharist is a concretion of what Christ is, then the discourse is properly called 'eucharistic', because what it is 'about', like much of the rest of the gospel, is Christ, in whom the flesh is submitted to the life-giving Spirit of God, and whose words consistently secure that submission.

It is at this point, the point of christology, that the vexed question of symbolism must arise, and Hoskyns himself introduces it when he comments: '*The living Bread* or *Flesh* is to the author of the gospel a comprehensive symbolical phrase containing a whole series of suggestions. It is to him what *Corpus Christi* is to the Catholic

Christian. Fundamentally it suggests the Christ incarnate, offered as a sacrifice, and finally glorified. It is then extended to embrace the regenerate believers who have been saved by the Christ. They are the true and living Bread which must not and indeed cannot be lost.'[2] The question is vexed because the word 'symbol' can be used in all manner of ill-defined ways, and in any case is not easy to define satisfactorily. In his *Symbolism and Belief*, Edwyn Bevan took as a starting-point Whitehead's definition of symbolism: 'The human mind is functioning symbolically when some components of its experience elicit consciousness, beliefs, emotions, and usages, respecting other components of its experience.'[3] He naturally wished to extend this definition, since as it stood it was concerned with human experience ordinarily understood to be constituting the whole of reality. He then distinguished two types of symbol: (i) that which stands for something of which we already have direct knowledge (like the Union Jack, which does not convey to the Briton any information about his country which he does not possess already); and (ii) that which purports to give information about the thing it symbolizes and to convey information about its nature (the instance he cites is of someone born blind having explained to him what the colour scarlet was by being told that it was like the sound of a trumpet. In the case of the first type the symbol need have no resemblance to what is symbolized (a Union Jack in no way resembles Britain), while in the case of the second type some measure of resemblance is essential. This is particularly so in the Fourth Gospel, where the 'signs' perform something of the function performed by parables in the other gospels. The physical event by its very shape and character provides an analogy of some aspect of the spiritual world. While the first type has some place in religion, especially in the cultus (bells, music etc.), it is the second with which theology will be concerned. Bevan made a further distinction between symbols which one can see behind, that is, one believes one can express the thought conveyed in other (possibly truer) terms, and symbols one cannot see behind, that is, the symbol is itself the nearest one can get to reality.

Two questions arise with reference to the language from which eucharistic symbolism is drawn. The first and more general question is of the validity of this way of thinking and of its claim to give information about what is symbolized – in this case the divine truth and divine action in Christ. This is partly a matter for the philosophy of religion and for the study of the psychology of symbolism.

The Eucharist and Symbolism in the New Testament

Such contribution as biblical theologians may make would seem to consist in their exhibiting to the best of their ability the biblical symbols in operation, in detecting their roots and development, their use and modification, and the experiences, influences, pressures and necessities under which these took place. Thus Austin Farrer, who constantly drew attention to images as the principal means of conveying truth in the Bible, argued that one of the effects of prophecy in Israel, with its judgment on idolatry and sin, was to separate the archetypal image, for example of God's rule in Israel, from its too human and fallible embodiment in David and his successors, and so to liberate it to express an eschatological hope for the future. Once this was done the question then was whether it was to persist simply as an abstract notion, a disembodied idea, or was to receive an adequate embodiment. The fulfilment of this hope in Christ he called a rebirth of images.[4] The matter is, however, complex, as any study of the background of the Fourth Gospel makes clear. The first centuries BC and AD were periods of considerable religious syncretism, from which the Jewish and early Christian traditions were not immune. Other influences than those which are generally called 'biblical' may have been at work. Thus, when in the Fourth Gospel the branches are said to abide in the vine, or the true bread is identified with the Son of Man who comes down from heaven, or the good shepherd knows and is known by his sheep etc., it is not easy to say how far an Old Testament symbol has been further extended and developed, or has been modified by the truth apprehended in Christ, or has been compounded with symbols derived from wider spheres than the Jewish or Jewish-Christian and expressive of religious experience and aspirations in the Hellenistic world.

The second and more particular question relates to the eucharist itself and its explication in liturgy. What symbolism is proper and essential to it, and by what criteria is this to be judged? If the eucharist were to be firmly established as essentially the Christian Passover, then this might provide the basis of selection of what symbols properly belong to it. But it cannot be so established. Both Paul and the Fourth Evangelist were prepared to detach from it the meal and to attach this to other symbols. Is the meal, then, to be regarded as the *sine qua non*, not only on grounds of dominical institution but also perhaps as one of the symbols we cannot get behind? But it is a symbolical meal whose essential reference is to who Christ is and what he does, and who Christ is and what he does are expressed in a wide range of christological symbols. Is the eucharist somehow to encompass them all, or are there limits to what it is expected to be and to do? Traditionally the church has attempted to solve this question in one or both of two ways, by having the eucharistic action set within the context of the reading of scripture, the creed and preaching, in which the christological affirmations are rehearsed and expounded, and by putting more and more of them into the eucharistic prayer itself. Neither can be undertaken now without encountering the acute problems which have emerged over the meaning and validity of the biblical language.

NOTES

1. E. C. Hoskyns and F. N. Davey, *The Fourth Gospel*, Faber 1947, pp.343ff.
2. Ibid., p.345.
3. E. Bevan, *Symbolism and Belief*, Fontana Books 1963, p.9.
4. See A. M. Farrer, *The Glass of Vision*, Dacre Press 1958, ch.vi, and his sermon on 'Messianic Prophecy and Preparation for Christ' in: A. M. Farrer et al., *The Communication of the Gospel in New Testament Times*, SPCK, pp.1ff.

5

Symbols and the Eucharist

Hugh Montefiore

Other contributors have been concerned with the *theology* of the eucharist. This essay is concerned with its *images and symbolic actions*. Wherein lies the difference?

C. G. Jung, in his *Symbols of Transformation*, identifies two different ways of thinking. One may be called directional thinking.

> If we scrutinize our thinking more closely still and follow out an intensive train of thought – the solution of a difficult problem for instance – we suddenly notice that we are *thinking in words*, that in very intensive thinking we begin talking to ourselves, or that we occasionally write down the problem or make a drawing of it, so as to be absolutely clear. Anyone who has lived for some time in a foreign country will certainly have noticed that after a while he begins to think in the language of that country. Any very intensive train of thought works itself out more or less in verbal form if, that is to say, one wants to express it, or teach it, or convince someone of it. To that extent, directed or logical thinking is reality-thinking, by means of which we initiate the successiveness of objectively real things, so that the images outside our mind follow one another in the same strictly causal sequence as the events taking place outside it. We also call this 'thinking with directed attention'.[1]

Jung notes that 'the material with which we think is *language* and *verbal concepts*, something which from time immemorial has been used as a bridge, and which has but a single purpose, namely that of communication.[2]

This leads Jung to go on to ask the further question – what happens when we do not think directedly? He answers: 'Our thinking then lacks all leading ideas and the sense of direction emanating from them. We no longer compel our thoughts along a definite track, but let them float, sink or rise according to their specific gravity.'[3] Jung quotes William James:[4]

> Much of our thinking consists of trains of images suggested one by another, of a sort of spontaneous reverie of which it seems likely enough that the higher brutes should be capable. This sort of thinking leads nevertheless to rational conclusions both practical and theoretical. As a rule, in this sort of irresponsible thinking the terms which come to be coupled together are empirical concretes, not abstractions.

Jung supplements James's definitions by adding:

> This sort of thinking does not tire us, it leads away from reality into fantasies of the past or future. At this point thinking in verbal form ceases, image piles on image, feeling on feeling... common speech calls this kind of thinking, dreaming.[5]

He attempts a summary as follows:

> We have therefore two kinds of thinking: directed thinking and dreaming or fantasy thinking. The former operates with speech elements for the purpose of communication, and is difficult and exhausting; the latter is effortless, working as it were spontaneously, with the contents ready to hand, and guided by unconscious motives. The one produces innovations and adaptation, copies reality and tries to act upon it; the other turns away from reality, sets free subjective tendencies, and, as regards adaptation, is unproductive.[6]

This distinction between directional thinking and fantasy thinking is fundamental to any understanding of the processes of human thought. The difference, however, must not be equated with that between conscious and unconscious thinking. Nor is the distinction absolute, for the two types of thinking are not mutually exclusive. There are many types of conscious thought which are not fully directional (in so far as they are not purely logical processes stripped of all affective elements) nor can they properly be called fantasy thinking, since they require concentration and effort, and include the apprehension of some form, order and concept. The reading and appreciation of poetry or art, or engagement in personal dialogue, are types of such 'mixed thinking'. An analysis of inspiration in both arts and sciences also suggests a fusion between these two ways of thinking.[7] This may perhaps underlie what Keats wrote to Benjamin Bailey: 'I have never yet been able to perceive how anything can be known for truth by consecutive reasoning.'[8]

It is within this area of 'mixed thinking' that 'worship thinking' properly lies. 'Worship thinking' is unique in as much as it is a corporate means of addressing and paying attention to God. It is to be distinguished from theology, which is directional thinking in conceptual terms about God. The Book of Revelation is a good example of 'worship thinking'. As Dr Farrer pointed out, at first sight it appears a product of fantasy thinking, but a closer study reveals that it has a firm structure and direction, and that it is the outcome of concentration and close attention.[9]

Jung, in the passage quoted above, goes on to suggest that directional thinking, which finds its apogee today in scientific reasoning, found expression in the Middle Ages in scholasticism:

> It consisted essentially in a dialectical gymnastics which gave the symbol of speech, the word, an absolute meaning, so that words came in the end to have a substantiality with which the ancients could invest their Logos only by attributing to it a mystical value. The great achievement of scholasticism was that it laid the foundation of a solidly built intellectual function, the *sine qua non* of modern science and technology.

It would not be appropriate here to examine how Luther's protest against this kind of scholastic thinking later developed into a type of Protestant scholasticism or how some more recent theologians reacted against 'the system' into various forms of theological existentialism. Nor does the present writer wish in any way to decry any serious attempt to examine the historical and literary origins of Christianity, or to articulate in logical terms the substance of the Christian faith: indeed he has tried to do these things himself. Yet the fact remains that, so far at least as the eucharist is concerned, such matters would seem to have little bearing on the experience or the consciousness of the ordinary worshipper as he shares in this central Christian rite. This is not to doubt the importance of such matters: but it is to doubt their relevance to the impact which a celebration of the eucharist has on its usual participants.

Of course, it is not easy to know what goes on in the minds and hearts of worshippers as they share in the holy communion. But it seems unlikely that (apart from intellectuals) many people conceptualize the words of the rite to any great extent. This is why heated arguments among theologians and liturgists over the precise verbal formulae used in the eucharistic prayers strike many laymen as irrelevant, except in so far as they feel threatened by even a verbal change. This is not to say that most lay people 'dream' their way through the eucharist (although some certainly do, because they are incapable of attention). On the contrary, Simone Weil has pointed out that 'absolutely unmixed attention is prayer'[10] and W. H. Auden has expanded her words as follows:[11]

> To pray is to pay attention to something or someone other than oneself. Whenever a man so concentrates his attention – on a landscape, a poem, a geometrical problem, an idol, or the True God – that he completely forgets his own ego and desires, he is praying. Choice of attention – to pay attention to this and not to that – is to the inner life what choice of action is to the outer.

To worship in the eucharist is to pay attention to God through the rite, and so to find oneself in a relationship of grace. It is not primarily to pay attention to the logic of the words but to use the images conveyed by the words and the symbolism of the ritual actions as means of paying attention to God.

It follows, therefore, that the type of thinking appropriate to worship is neither directional thinking – for we use personal language in our approach to God, to which logical thinking, stripped of all subjective elements is unsuited – nor is it day-dreaming, since that would mean self-absorption, whereas the essence of worship is to take attention away from ourselves and to give it to God. 'Worship thinking' (to coin a phrase) is rather a combination of elements from both these other two ways of thinking. There must be a logical structure for worship, because we are to offer to God 'our very selves, a living sacrifice, dedicated and fit for his acceptance, the worship offered by mind and heart' (Rom. 12.1). But when we feel that we have been present at a particularly real and significant act of worship, we do not mean that we have been specially attentive to an act of theological ratiocination, but that we have been enabled to use what has been said and done as a way of entering into a real relationship of grace with God. If we had merely been day-dreaming, our hearts and minds would, by free association, have moved farther and farther from God into fantasy.

But the spoken images and enacted symbols of the rite, which form the jumping-off point for day-dreaming, can be controlled by the will so that they, together with all the rich devotional associations – conscious or unconscious – which they evoke, become the vehicle for an act of profound attention to God through Christ. It is such an act of attention to which people generally refer when they say that a particular occasion of worship was specially significant for them. Directive thinking is in essence an active process demanding that the full attention of the mind be given to the process of discursive reasoning and giving little outlet to the imagination or the feelings. Ratiocination about God (or theology) cannot therefore be a proper means of addressing God, nor is it likely to appeal to the non-intellectual Christian. 'Worship thinking', however, while it requires the direction of the will to keep intellect, feelings and imagination within certain limits (in contrast to fantasy thinking) is in itself a more passive process of reflexion, in which the mind dwells on images and symbolic actions, thereby enabling attention through them to be given to God. It demands full concentration on the part of the worshipper, yet it is within ordinary human capacity because it does not require any special intellectual powers. Because we are human beings with the human ability to conceptualize, we have a natural desire to form concepts about God. But God cannot be confined within a concept, and so theology needs not only the *via analogica* but also the *via negativa* in straining to express the inexpressible. 'Worship thinking', however, is not primarily conceptual thinking: it is a process of reflection on images and symbolic actions as a means of paying attention to God who lies beyond them as well as acting through them: and so it awakens the worshipper to the sense of the numinous by directing attention to the transcendence as well as to the immanence of God.

Images and symbols therefore have a far greater significance for worship, and for the evaluation of what actually happens when people worship, than most theologians and liturgists have realized. In the scriptures 'the stuff of inspiration is living images'.[12] Not so in some modern liturgies. Thus in Series II holy communion, the brevity and terseness so appropriate to Latin collects predominates throughout the rite, so that, for all its merits, it lacks the richness of image and symbol which help to make the old Cranmerian liturgy so greatly beloved. A Liturgical Commission needs to be as clear about the nature and function of 'worship thinking' as about the details of liturgical structure and eucharistic theology. Happily there are signs that this lesson is being learnt. Series III holy communion is wealthier in symbol and image than Series II.

The Christian sacraments are particularly rich in images and symbolic actions, partly because they are not primarily said but done, in as much as they are performed by means of symbolic acts, and partly because the outward visible sign in the sacrament provides a link with the natural world which enables it to be rich in conscious or unconscious associations. F. W. Dillistone[13] cites in this connection the words of Paul Tillich.[14]

> Are we still able to understand what a sacrament means? The more we are estranged from Nature, the less we can answer affirmatively. That is why, in our time, the sacraments have lost so much of their significance for individuals and Churches. For in the sacraments Nature participates in the process of salvation. Bread and wine, water and light, and all the great elements of Nature become the bearers of spiritual meaning and saving power. Natural and spiritual powers are united – reunited – in the sacrament. The word appeals to our intellect and may move our will. The sacrament, if the meaning is alive, grasps our unconscious as well as our conscious being. It grasps the creative ground of our being.

The effect of the spoken images and symbolic actions upon the individual is to a large extent subjective; and it may be theologically good or theologically bad, harmful or beneficial to the individual psyche. Two illustrations may be given from pastoral experience. Many parishes, after the introduction of Series II, had a period of trial and experiment before deciding that the new service should be substituted for the old. The present writer recollects many hours spent in introducing the new rite to his congregation, many attempts at theological explanation, many weeks of experiment. Finally the decision had to be made. Strangely there was only one objection, non-theological but very strongly held. 'Vicar, at last I know what we don't like: we've lost the gospel procession.' The symbolic action of facing the gospel of Christ, of focussing light upon the gospel in the midst of the people, meant more to that congregation than any new verbal formula introduced into the prayer of thanksgiving. The continuance of this action, although hard to devise, seemed essential to make. It was what it signified: it brought inward light and renewal; it was a means of grace. The congregation found it hard to pinpoint their earlier objection to the rite, probably because they were unable to verbalize the meaning of this symbolic action: they had simply accepted it and found it life-giving. No doubt their reasons for this were subjective, dependent on that to which they had become habituated. But if God spoke to them thus, it was for them a real means of grace.

A second example shows how symbolic actions can be bad in their effect. The present writer recalls another occasion when, with the consent of his church council, he introduced a nave altar at the parish communion. At the conclusion of the service a normally pious and peaceful lady left the church shaking her fist at him, shouting, 'You've taken away my long walk to God'. Now, whatever the transcendence of God may signify, God in Christ does come to meet us: we do not have to walk to him. And yet the symbolic act of walking from the back pew to the high altar had been tremendously important to this lady. Perhaps it had helped to satisfy her need to keep God at a distance? At all events, without it she felt deeply threatened; so threatened that for the first time she had been able to formulate its importance to her. This second illustration not merely shows the importance of symbolic acts in the eucharist, but also their potentiality for doing as much harm as good, since their significance may be so different for each individual. This underlines the need for an adequate sacramental theology to control the words and actions of the eucharistic rite and also, if necessary, to correct or nullify any harmful associations which these words and acts may have for an individual.

Different schools of psychoanalysis differ in their interpretation of symbols, but they are all agreed on their importance. So far as the Christian sacraments are concerned, one does not have to subscribe to Jung's theory of archetypes to hold that they can speak to all men in as much as they make use of universal symbols.

The use of symbols and rituals in a religious context has recently been examined by a distinguished anthropologist in her Scott Holland lectures.[15] Dr Wilson confines for her purposes the meaning of ritual to the symbolic relationships between man and what is conceived of as transcendental reality. 'Religion is not confined in ritual, but it is manifest in ritual.'[16] Rituals compel the expression of certain attitudes.[17] She notes that during periods of rapid change consciousness of symbolism diminishes. 'Ritual draws sanctity from antiquity but it must be felt relevant to the celebrant's world.'[18] None the less, rituals are generally understood in the societies in which they obtain. 'The symbols used in ritual are public not private. Their function is to communicate.... They may coincide with private symbols revealed in psychoanalysis ... but private imaginings go beyond set forms.'[19] The power of symbol and ritual in the eucharist is precisely that it makes use, in a set form, of universal symbols and ritual actions. It might seem at first sight as though the meaning given and the associations evoked by spoken images and symbolic acts are so subjective that it is impossible to generalize about them. This is not the case. Despite individual variations, the universal meaning of symbols of the eucharist can be generally understood, although their religious associations are increasingly lost on a society becoming alienated from religious belief and practice.

It is interesting to note that the symbols and images of the eucharist receive much more prominence in eucharistic hymns than in the words of the rite, and perhaps this accounts in part for their popularity. We have already remarked on the use of light in connection with the eucharist at the gospel procession; a universal religious symbol, as reflected in the hymn:

> Sun, who all my life dost brighten
> Light, who dost my soul enlighten ...

Light symbolizes glory, warmth, and inward illumination. It can 'spotlight' or 'highlight' a key moment.

The money offered during the eucharist has also a symbolic aspect. Money shows that we mean business: it is a token of possessions, power and personal self-offering. The fact that it is associated in offering with the bread and wine to be consecrated, and that it is often placed upon the holy table, suggests that the rite is concerned with the sanctification of ordinary lives, which ordinary people offer to God for renewal.

The table itself is a potent symbol of fellowship and food. It suggests a host, a meal, a fellowship or family and as such it often finds a mention in eucharistic hymns:

> Author of life divine,
>   Who has a table spread ...
> O let thy table honoured be
>   And furnished well with joyful guests ...

But as well as being a natural symbol, the table also has religious associations with sacrifice, so that it is set apart as 'the holy table':

Symbols and the Eucharist

> And so we show thy death, O Lord,
> Till thou again appear,
> And feel when we approach thy board
> We have an altar here.

In fact the potency of eucharistic symbols is that they are natural symbols acquiring additional force and meaning from their religious context; and this again often appears in hymns. St Thomas Aquinas had an austere and scholastic sacramental theology, but when he turned his hand to verse his power lay in his adroit combination of symbolic language.

> By birth their fellow-man was he,
> Their meat, when sitting at the board;
> He died, their ransomer to be;
> He ever reigns, their great reward.

Among the most vivid images used during the service are the 'cherubim and seraphim and all the company of heaven'. No one knows what cherubim and seraphim are supposed to look like, and this gives free rein to the imagination. But they are creatures who belong to the supernatural world; and the image is so important because it imports a feeling of transcendence: it helps the worshipper to feel that he is linked here on earth with the courts of heaven:

> Let all mortal flesh keep silence
> And with fear and trembling stand ...
> Rank on rank the host of heaven
> Spreads its vanguard on the way ...
> At his feet the six winged seraphs,
> Cherubim with sleepless eye,
> Veil their faces to the presence ...

None of these images or symbols is absolutely essential to the service. The only two necessary elements, which traditionally constitute the form of the sacrament, are bread and wine. Both are so potent because they are natural symbols with an added religious significance.

The offering of bread and wine is a symbol of hospitality. It is a very deeply felt and almost universal instinct that a true welcome shows itself in offering food and drink. And so the very fact that a sacred meal lies at the centre of the rite demonstrates the generous acceptance by God of his people. We eat and drink as his guests:

> There with joy thy praises render
> Unto him whose grace unbounded
> Hath this wondrous banquet founded ...

But before we can receive bread and wine at his hands, we have to offer it to him so that it may become the symbol of our renewal. This offering is a kind of miniature harvest festival, and lying behind it are the 'types and shadows' of numberless fertility rites finding their focus in this God-given sacrament. It is another deeply felt human instinct to return to the donor part of his present as a thanksgiving for the whole. So in the eucharistic rite it is a symbolic act to give back to God a token of our sustenance as a sign of our thanks.

Bread is a natural symbol for the satisfaction of need. 'He feeds the hungry with the bread of heaven.' 'The hungry soul would feed on thee.' Bread is *ordinary* food, a symbol of day-to-day sustenance: 'Thou, on earth, our food, our stay.' At reception of communion, we lift up needy hands to be fed: the action is symbolic of the hunger of our souls. (In certain traditions, the recipient opens his mouth to be fed, like a fledgeling that cannot fend for itself fed by the parent bird.) Food, however, does not merely signify the relief of need. An infant, long before he can reason, associates nourishment with comfort, pleasure and a loving relationship:

> O Lord Jesus, I adore thee
> For the bread of worth untold
> Freely given in thy Communion,
> Wonderful a thousandfold.
> Given today in loving bounty
> More than my poor heart can hold.

There is probably a symbolic aspect to the *amount* of bread received at the communion: it is almost as if it were a homeopathic dose, a white tablet of *pharmakon athanasiās*, the medicine of immortality. Even this symbol finds its way into hymnody:

> And by this food, so awful and so sweet,
> Deliver us from every touch of ill ...

Linked with this natural symbolism there are specially religious associations connected with the passion of Jesus. The breaking of bread may have originally been a sign of hospitality, but the action soon became connected – unbiblically[20] – with the broken body of Christ:

Symbols and the Eucharist

> Bread of the world in mercy broken,
> Wine of the soul in mercy shed,
> By whom the deeds of life were spoken,
> And in whose death our sins are dead.

The bread becomes the bread of heaven: it is everlasting bread, because it is none other than Christ himself. The food it contains is the 'life imparting heavenly manna' which is Christ himself.

> Bread of heaven on thee we feed,
> For thy flesh is meat indeed.
> Ever may our souls be fed
> With this true and living bread,
> Day by day with strength supplied,
> Through the life of him who died.

Thus the use of bread and the actions connected with it in the eucharist not merely use natural and universal symbols, but also add to them religious associations which are expressed in those myths and rites of the ancient world which entail 'eating the god' and which find their meaning and reality in the death of Jesus and the 'benefits of his passion'.

The same, generally speaking, is true of the cup and the wine. Wine is a natural symbol of feast and festival. If bread is typical of ordinary nourishment, wine is the token of the special occasion. It expresses and encourages cheerfulness and conviviality: it is 'wine that maketh glad the heart of man'. Men do not usually drink wine alone: the cup symbolizes a party, a common meal, whether among friends or within the family. The shared cup symbolizes the unity of believers in Christ, just as a loving cup at a feast is meant to express the conviviality of the occasion. (The shared cup is a more dramatic symbol than the 'one loaf', partly because it is seen by all communicants, and partly because the 'one loaf' may in fact consist of a heap of individual wafers.)

The cup in the Bible not only symbolizes joy and happiness, but also suffering and pain. The eucharistic wine – usually red – is a symbol of the blood of Christ. There is a fusion of images. Blood symbolizes life, for without blood we cannot live. To drink the wine is a symbolic act of sharing in the life-blood of Christ. Blood, however, symbolizes not only life but death; for blood outpoured, unless staunched, leads to death. And so to drink the consecrated wine is not merely to share in the life-blood of Christ but also to assert his sacrificial death. One image leads to another: images become fused.

Since the blood-shedding of Jesus is sacrificial, it cleanses (like a lustration); it reconciles (like a piaculum); it makes holy (like a sacrificium). The image of the eucharistic chalice thus not only generates feelings of festival, friendship and unity; it fuses these with feelings of cleansing, reconciliation and sanctification.

Once again natural and universal symbols are used and made potent with religious associations. In this case these religious symbols have affinities with those myths and rites of the ancient world which may be summed up by the word sacrifice, and again which find their meaning and reality in the death of Jesus and the 'benefits of his passion'. Once again the feelings generated by symbol and image are illustrated better by hymns than by theological exposition:

> O stream of love unending,
>   Poured from the one true Vine,
> With our weak nature blending
>   The strength of life divine;
> Our thankful faith confessing
>   In thy life-blood outpoured,
> We drink this cup of blessing
>   And praise thy name, O Lord.

The bread and the wine of the eucharist may possibly have a further symbolic significance. The psychology of mourning has begun to be investigated in depth.[21] In particular the use of inanimate objects, adopted and utilized by pathological mourners, has been the subject of research.[22] There is a persistent seeking for reunion with the lost one; and the linking objects – which are to be distinguished from fetishes or 'transitional objects' – are adopted as symbols in order to keep a link with the dead. It is dangerous to argue from pathological to normal states; but it is at least possible that the psychological mechanism (and the symbols associated with it) of pathological mourners are not unconnected with the way in which the believer feels linked with Jesus through the use of bread and wine. It is true that, theologically speaking, the link is with the risen and living Lord, not with the dead Jesus, but psychologically speaking (as the 1662 rite shows) it is often the dead Jesus who predominates in the rite and to whom reference can be found made in hymns:

> O blessed memorial of our dying Lord.

At the beginning of this essay a distinction was made between direc-

Symbols and the Eucharist

ted thinking, fantasy thinking and what was called 'worship thinking'. An attempt has been made to identify some of the symbols and images of the eucharist and the feelings and sentiments with which they are generally associated. It was emphasized near the outset that an analysis of worship thinking is not intended to supplant eucharistic thology: on the contrary, eucharistic theology is essential. In the first place it is required in order to direct and guide the way in which people are to understand the meaning of the eucharist. In the second place it vindicates the use of a particular image or symbolic action within the context of the eucharist as a whole; and thirdly, an important function of eucharistic theology is to produce a coherent strand of language which licenses the use and combination of different images and symbolic actions within the one rite.

None the less, it is not by means of eucharistic theology but through the images and symbolic actions of the eucharist that people are able to pay attention to God in Christ; and it is part of the God-given structure of the rite that natural images are given religious overtones and associations. A change of emphasis through symbolic action (such as standing in a circle to receive communion, or laying the table at the offertory) can re-orient the rite far more than an alteration in the theological wording of an eucharistic prayer. (Incidentally, the function of image and symbol in other fields of theology, e.g. New Testament theology, particularly in St John's Gospel, would repay deeper investigation.) Most important of all, it is not so much through acts of sacramental reasoning but by using these eucharistic images and symbolic acts that man receives grace and is enabled to respond to God in the sacrament of holy communion.

NOTES

1. C. G. Jung, *Symbols of Transformation*, Routledge and Kegan Paul ²1967, p.11.
2. Ibid., p.12.
3. Ibid., p.17.
4. William James, *Principles of Psychology*, Constable n.d., vol.II, p.325.
5. Jung, op. cit., p.16.
6. Ibid., p.18.
7. Cf. R. E. M. Harding, *An Anatomy of Inspiration*, Cambridge University Press 1940.
8. Letter to Benjamin Bailey, 22 November 1817.
9. A. M. Farrer, *The Revelation of St John the Divine*, Oxford University Press 1964, pp.23ff.

10. Simone Weil, *Gravity and Grace*, Routledge and Kegan Paul 1952, p.106.
11. W. H. Auden, *A Certain World*, Faber 1971, p.306.
12. A. M. Farrer, *The Glass of Vision*, Dacre Press 1948, p.44.
13. F. W. Dillistone, *Christianity and Symbolism*, Collins 1955, p.288.
14. Paul Tillich, *The Shaking of the Foundations*, SCM Press 1949, p.86.
15. M. Wilson, *Religion and the Transformation of Society*, Cambridge University Press 1971.
16. Ibid., p.52.
17. Ibid., p.58.
18. Ibid., p.75.
19. Ibid., pp.57f.
20. See John 19.36.
21. Cf. J. Bowlby, 'Processes of Mourning', *International Journal of Psychoanalysis* 42, 1961, pp.317ff.; L. D. Siggins, 'Mourning: A Critical Survey of the Literature', *IJP* 47, 1966, pp.14ff.
22. Cf. V. D. Volcan, 'The Linking Objects of Pathological Mourners', an unpublished paper read at the Fall meeting of the American Psychoanalytical Association in December 1970; I am grateful to Dr Dorothy Heard for drawing my attention to this.

6

Sacrifice and the Eucharist[1]

J. L. Houlden

The aim of this essay is to clarify a cloudy area in the landscape of Christian theology; then to see whether the name by which it has traditionally been known, eucharistic sacrifice, remains a candidate for survival. We begin by examining the substructure of the problem: what makes talk of sacrifice in relation to the eucharist so laden with difficulty? This leads to the question: what was there in Jewish sacrificial institutions that brought this language into play in relation to Christ and his acts? The third and longest section of the essay is devoted to an attempt to disentangle the great number of conceptual threads in the use of sacrificial language in eucharistic theology in the course of the church's history. Finally, we face the question: what needs to be said? Does the language of sacrifice aid the saying of it?

1. *The Substructure*

Most obviously, difficulty arises because the image of sacrifice is no longer current coin. The institution belongs, as far as Christian use is concerned, to ancient Israel, and parallels in currently flourishing religions have only a rather remote anthropological interest for Christians living in the West and indeed in many other parts of the world.

But while this difficulty reduces the vividness of the language, it is partly curable by instruction. More serious is the fact that as we survey the history of Christian doctrine we find that there is no one, clearly identifiable entity which we can label 'the doctrine of eucharistic sacrifice'. As we shall see, the term has covered a wide variety of ideas, many of them having hardly any relation to each other and operating along quite distinct logical lines. So we have to ask: what precisely is being discussed when this terminology is used?

It is common in discussion of this, as of other theological topics, for hidden Platonist assumptions to cause much needless confusion, and the fact that a particular phrase has had a number of different senses sometimes merely intensifies the tenacity with which these assumptions are held. The supposed objective existence of something called 'the eucharistic sacrifice' easily diverts attention from haziness about the meaning. Statements such as 'I understand *the* eucharistic sacrifice thus and thus' or 'I see *it* so and so' conceal the fact that the term is being stretched to cover a wide range of concepts, and that distinctions are crying out to be made.

This diversity of sense is of course a feature, to one degree or another, of the history of every Christian doctrine. There are, for instance, many christologies, many doctrines of the atonement. But in the case of eucharistic sacrifice, it is accentuated by uncertainty as to what precisely is at stake. We may draw a contrast. Thus, in the case of christology, it is clear that whatever formulation is adopted, it is an attempt to give an account of the belief that in the person of Jesus there is a special or unique meeting of divine and human. In the case of the atonement, there is always an attempt to show how Christ's work may be understood as restoring alienated man to relationship with God. That is what christology and atonement doctrine are about. In the case of eucharistic sacrifice, there is no comparably specific task. It is simply that Christians have traditionally used the language of sacrifice in relation to the eucharist, though their intention in doing so has been to give expression to a wide range of quite distinct ideas concerning the sacrament.

We shall see that the ideas which enter into the discussion of this doctrine include some that are not strictly theological at all, and some that depend upon the wording of a particular biblical or liturgical text, written usually with other purposes in mind. It is not hard to see why eucharistic doctrine has displayed this luxuriant quality to a far greater degree than, for example, christology or atonement doctrine. It has had to make its way through the conceptually loose growth of liturgical and devotional formulae as well as the more tightly controlled paths marked out by councils and theologians. In sum, 'eucharistic sacrifice' has covered a multifarious variety of ideas which have in common little more than (*a*) some element of Godward movement of thought or aspiration, and (*b*) a link with some aspect of the eucharist. A number of them have had little to do with what we shall refer to as the central eucharistic 'area', that is the features, grounded in the Last Supper, which distinguish the eucharist from other rites and acts. Nevertheless, it is not right to suppose that the idea of sacrifice has been imposed upon the eucharist: rather, it has been drawn out of it – in a variety of ways, some more appropriate than others.

2. The Background

The language of sacrifice came into Christian vocabulary from the already diversified practice of Judaism. There, sacrificial rites ranged from the peace offerings (in which the animal was partly burned on the altar as 'food offered by fire for a pleasing odour' and partly consumed by the people, in a fellowship meal between God and his people) to sin offerings and burnt offerings (in which there was no meal, and the rite signified total consecration to God, or, in the case of the former, brought release from sin). Passover, which lay more immediately in the background of Christ's death and so of the Last Supper, though not itself a rite belonging to any of these categories, combined a number of their themes. The eating of this meal in Jewish households was the expression *par excellence* of the harmonious communion between Israel and God. It expressed the proper and total allegiance of the people to God their redeemer; and it saw this as grounded in the historic act of deliverance from Egypt.

It was not long before the first Christians, experiencing reconciliation to God as a result of Christ's life, death and resurrection, began to interpret their experience in the language closest to hand, that of sacrifice. The underlying logic was simple: reconciliation had taken place, sacrifices reconcile, so Christ's work, the occasion and basis of the reconciliation, must be interpreted sacrificially. There was less agreement about the precise application of this range of imagery. The New Testament writers show three chief patterns. Attention naturally focussed on Christ's death (for sacrificial victims die), and it was easy to see it as the once for ever effective sin-offering (e.g. Rom. 3.24f.). If, as in the Epistle to the Hebrews, the ritual of the Day of Atonement was chosen as the model, then Christ's sacrifice was seen as consummated at his entry into heaven, by analogy with the high priest entering the holy of holies in the temple. In the gospels (e.g. in the symbolism of the Fourth Gospel and perhaps in Mark 10.45), Jesus' death was not surprisingly seen in the light of the Passover rite, for it occurred at the time of the feast: it effected perfectly and universally what that rite signified for Israel – a profound deliverance from all bondage, to be completed in the messianic kingdom. But whatever the pattern, it comes to this: that God was seen to have acted in Christ in a manner most satisfactorily expounded in sacrificial terms, and this act had met and made realizable the desire of alienated man for fellowship with his Creator.

It was the most natural thing in the world that the liturgical act, whereby Christ's death is recalled and made once more vivid to his people, and whereby eternal fellowship with God is anticipated, should also attract to itself sacrificial language and imagery. What is perhaps surprising is the tortuous and complex way in which this has often been done. This will be apparent, as we go on to examine the story of the church's use of the idea of sacrifice in connection with the eucharist.

3. *The Story*

What now follows is not primarily intended to be a chronological summary of the history of ideas in relation to eucharistic sacrifice, but rather a survey of the different patterns of thought which have arisen in this area. For the sake of clarity, we shall occasionally sharpen distinctions a little unfairly. The chief aim is to provide analysis. The result will be threefold. First, to rule some of the ideas out of strictly doctrinal discussion altogether – they belong in the less rigorous sphere of aids to devotion. Whether they are misleading or helpful is a question to be judged by other criteria, those proper to that sphere. Second, to show some as so wedded to outdated or barren conceptual and symbolic patterns as to be overripe for relegation to the museum for religious period-pieces. Third, to make clearer the terms on which discussion can now usefully be conducted.

The following list of twelve distinguishable strands is unlikely to be exhaustive. But it may be long enough both for the reader's patience and to demonstrate the main point of this essay.

1. *First signs*. The root of the matter is in Mal. 1.11, a text which speedily commended itself to Christian expositors who saw the fulfilment of the Old Testament in the deeds of Christ and the preaching of the church. It does not appear in any of the New Testament books, but was certainly in use before the last of them was written. The verse is: 'From the rising of the sun to its setting my name is great among the nations, and in every place incense is offered to my name, and a pure offering; for my name is great among the nations, says the Lord of hosts.'

It makes its first appearance in the *Didache of the Twelve Apostles* (ch.14), where the stress is on the need for a *pure* sacrifice and the quotation backs an exhortation not to take part in the eucharist until personal differences have been settled. Moral purity is a prerequisite for worship. There is no stress whatsoever on the term 'sacrifice' itself, and the context is not theological but hortatory. This writer's typical way of describing the eucharist is as the breaking of bread and the giving of thanks (cf. also *Did.* 9). Nevertheless, the text – and the word 'sacrifice' – had gained a foothold in Christian speech about the eucharist.

In other writers, the text comes into prominence for three other reasons. In the first place, it was part of a set of Old Testament passages with liturgical connections, which were seen as foretelling in various ways the contrast between the purely Jewish old Israel, with its inadequate worship, and the new universal church. The use of Isa. 56.7 (cf. also Jer. 7.11) in Mark 11.17 is perhaps the first instance of this: 'My house shall be called a house of prayer for all the nations.' The vein came to be richly worked, for example, in the second century, in Justin's *Dialogue with Trypho* (41,117), where, in addition to use of the Malachi text, it is explored in relation to circumcision and the sabbath. In the second place, the text enables a writer like Justin to underline the providential universality of the church. The fact that it was possible to point to a contrast, between Israel's sacrifice confined to Jerusalem and the church's which was found 'in every place', enabled Justin to by-pass a fact inconvenient for apologetic – that Jews as well as Christians were to be found throughout the cities of the Roman world (cf. also Irenaeus, *Against Heresies*, IV.17.5).

In the third place, the theme of sacrifice forms one element in a typological scheme which speedily emerged in the thought-patterns of the early church. By this, the people of the new covenant are seen to possess a set of 'equipment' parallel at each point to that possessed by the people of the old. In this case, it is as if it was said: 'they had their sacrifices, we have ours, for sacrifice is part of the providentially ordered scheme'. This line of thought is first worked out at the end of the first century in the *First Epistle of Clement* (40.4), which also includes the similar parallel between the priesthood of Israel and the officers of the church: 'The High Priest has his own proper services assigned to him.... In the same way, my brothers, when we offer our own Eucharist to God, each one of us should keep to his own degree.' A century later, Irenaeus repeats the argument: 'There were oblations there (among the Jews), and there are oblations here (among the Christians)' (IV.18.2). It is evident that it is the presence of sacrifices in the religious institutions of Israel which impels the application of this language to the most closely comparable element among the institutions of the church, to wit, the eucharist, rather than anything demanded by the nature of the eucharist itself. The argument began with the old rather than the new, and the old called the tune.

The most interesting feature of the early uses of this text is that from the point of view of doctrinal thinking and the emergence of a concept of eucharistic sacrifice, every one of these aspects is quite incidental. Of all the elements in Mal. 1.11, the idea of sacrifice in itself was the least explored of all, in the period when it was so prominently employed. It may not be going too far to say that in many cases, the term 'sacrifice' carries little or nothing of its technical sense. It signifies hardly more than *Gottesdienst, l'office, religious service* do with us, that is, it is the quite general term for an act of religious worship, and does not indicate any particular way of looking at the eucharist.

2. *Offering gifts*. From early times, the element of sacrifice in the eucharist has been seen in terms of 'offering the gifts'. It seems to have arisen as part of the typological pattern which we referred to above (p.85). Its first appearance was in *I Clement* 44.4, where, quite casually it seems, the essential office of the bishop is described in these terms: 'For we shall be guilty of no slight sin if we eject from the episcopate men who have offered the gifts blamelessly and holily.' Once more then the language of sacrifice is a subsidiary feature. It was nourished by the appeal to other Old Testament texts besides Mal. 1.11, in particular Deut. 16.16. This appears, for example, in Irenaeus (*Against Heresies* IV.18.1): 'We are bound, therefore, to offer to God the firstfruits of his creation, as Moses also says, "Thou shalt not appear in the presence of the Lord thy God empty-handed"; so that man, being accounted as grateful, by those things in which he has shown his gratitude, may receive that honour which flows from him.' (Cf. also Justin's seeing of the Jewish offering of fine flour by those purified from leprosy as a foreshadowing of the eucharistic bread, *Dialogue with Trypho* 41.)

Without this typological frame of mind, it is hard to see how the idea would have come into the eucharistic 'area', with which it is not at all integrally connected. At no point does it link conceptually with the eucharist's central concern, that is, with the Lord's death and resurrection and his people's status in relation to him. The typological mentality created a feeling of deep inner appropriateness, linking old offering with new, which pushed its way to the surface in reflection upon the eucharist, as upon other matters. The rite was, after all, one might say, the most likely candidate within Christian practice for such treatment in relation to this theme. But it is so unspecifically eucharistic that it could equally appropriately be attached to quite other Christian devotions, e.g. harvest festivals or gift days. Moreover, the insistent objection presents itself, that God has no need of our gifts and that the underlying conception is, from the point of view of Christian belief about God, crude and mistaken. Nevertheless, once this idea had found an entry into Christian thought on the eucharist, it was hard to dislodge, and has had enthusiastic revivals in recent years.

3. *Firstfruits of creation.* This is a special form of the idea which we have just examined and suffers from the same defects. But it brings its own special associations. The bread and wine are presented to God as the first instalments of a creation, which one day will be wholly rejuvenated. Irenaeus expresses it thus (IV.18.4): 'For it behoves us to make an oblation to God, and in all things to be found grateful to God our Maker, in a pure mind, and in faith without hypocrisy, in well-grounded hope, and in fervent love, offering the firstfruits of his own created things.' He goes on to attack those who see the created order as having issued from 'apostasy, ignorance and passion', in these words: 'How can they be consistent with themselves, when they say that the bread over which thanks have been given is the body of their Lord, and the cup his blood, if they do not call him the Son of the creator of the world, that is, his Word, through whom the wood fructifies, and the fountains gush forth, and the earth gives "first the blade, then the ear, then the full corn in the ear".'

Obviously this idea is full of rich devotional content But it is only marginally linked with the meaning of the eucharist and has no clear connection with the idea of sacrifice in relation to the eucharistic 'area', as we defined it on p.83.

4. *The offering of Christ's body and blood.* A successor to and crucial variant of the idea of *offering gifts* arises when, in Cyprian, the notion of offering is weaned from its predominantly typological context and attached more closely to other – and more central – aspects of eucharistic belief, in particular the presence in the sacrament of Christ's Body and Blood. The fusion results, as it were

haphazardly, in the following concept: that of offering to God as our gifts the body and blood of Christ.[2]

From the point of view of the logic of doctrine, this is the key moment in the development of the idea of eucharistic sacrifice. Ideas about Godward offering, making use, as we have seen, of a variety of sacrificial notions, mostly drawn from the Old Testament, but all of them peripheral to the content and meaning of the eucharist, now win a place in the centre of the picture, through the association of sacrificial language with 'body and blood' language. The latter had so far had a separate history and had always belonged to the very heart of the eucharistic 'area'.

Yet surely this marriage was a mistake. The life and death of Jesus are past events. Jesus offered himself on the cross. Present Christian life is 'in Christ', and is offered to God only by its relation to Christ's self-offering. It could never do justice to those facts and ideas to describe any Christian act as *our* offering of Christ's body and blood to the Father. It presented the relationship of Christ and Christian as too external and inevitably threatened to treat the 'body and blood' as manipulable objects. Moreover, it failed to do full justice to the eucharist as the expression of an already existing relationship of the believers with God through Christ. It is all the more tragic, then, that all subsequent development was to be within the context of this fusion and to be bedevilled by it. However widely thought about eucharistic sacrifice was to range, it always stayed within the terms which it laid down – whether by way of working out its implications in the light of some new doctrinal emphasis or intellectual setting, or by way of reaction against it.

5. *Propitiation and Satisfaction.* Under the former heading (i.e. the working out of the implications of the idea of *offering Christ's body and blood*) we may place the most important new emphasis of the succeeding period. It is the effect upon eucharistic belief of that stringent sense of God's justice and its requirements which is associated particularly with the name of Anselm (though it goes back much earlier, even perhaps to Cyprian, the lawyer turned bishop), and which is best seen as one element in a general concern in the medieval period with the establishing and defining of legal rights and obligations. Once the whole question of Christ's redemptive work was set in the context of a God whose inflexible justice was an overriding characteristic, the sacrifice of the eucharist was bound to take on a new aspect and to raise new questions. Fresh elements in the ample stock (from both scripture and the Christian

tradition) of sacrificial terminology pressed to the forefront of men's minds.

In particular, there was the question of the relationship between the past, all-sufficing act of satisfaction for sin made on the cross and the repeated act of the eucharist. The two acts clearly bore so many of the same characteristics, and demanded to be spoken of in closely similar terms. Above all, both alike were rich in sacrificial associations. How, then, was the relationship to be defined? Could the first avail for man by means of the second? In the search for definition, various possibilities were exploited. The three leading ones may be expressed in the form of propositions: (i) 'The daily sacrifice is a *memorial* of the *Passion*' (Paschasius Radbertus, ninth century); (ii) 'Christ is daily immolated *mystically*' (ibid.); (iii) The eucharist is an *unbloody* sacrifice. The italicized words show the points at which the statement is most vulnerable or ambiguous, as if it were attempting at the same time to say and refrain from saying, working towards precision but not quite attaining it. In each case, the concern is to establish both the connection and the distinction between the cross and the eucharist, the one 'sacrifice' and the other. In the light of later controversy (from the fifteenth century onwards), the first way of expressing this (in terms of *memorial*) looks a good deal weaker than the other two; but it is not clear that when they were first formulated it was seen as essentially different from them.

All these expressions bear chiefly on the *kind* of sacrifice that the eucharist was thought to be. There was also the question of how the sacrifice was to be seen to work. How did the past act affect present life, and how did the eucharist operate to that end? There were two chief lines of approach. The first and older was in terms of *propitiation*. Taken from Jewish precedents, it was applied (or taken to have been applied) to the death of Jesus in the teaching of St Paul and St John (Rom. 3.25 and I John 2.2). It had been applied to the eucharist from the time of Cyril of Jerusalem in the fourth century. In the context of the medieval assumptions, questions and demands, this was the most appropriate category available within the traditional theological vocabulary of sacrifice.

But more immediate to men's minds and more powerful psychologically, was the category of satisfaction, with its roots in the assumptions of society, in particular those of feudalism. Men were deeply conscious that in coming before the all-holy, perfectly just God, payment must be made of all outstanding dues. Man could not come to God without the required payment for his sins – or a commutation of it. Just as knight-service could be commuted into a money payment, so the sacrifice of Christ could be commuted into the offering of the eucharistic elements.

In a variant of the same idea, the sacrifice could be offered with a view to achieving certain objects; for the forgiveness of sins, or for the obtaining of specified benefits. As the history of the Roman canon shows, this approach indeed antedated both the atonement theory of Anselm which gave it the most comprehensive formal backing and the social system whose demands made it so fitting.[3] By this time, the eucharist had long been regarded by many as an *effective* sacrifice, with purchasing power for the needs of both the living and the dead. Once more, this was a feature in eucharistic thinking that was peripheral to the rite's distinctive and central significance, for intercession, thanksgiving and penitence can be expressed quite apart from the eucharist. But that act was felt to be the occasion when the worshipper could with most confidence bring his petitions, for it was his closest approach to the heart of the majesty of God. Christ, who had made the perfect sacrifice, would plead its merits, as the worshipper's friendly advocate at the heavenly court.

6. *The sacrifice of Jesus: human and once for all*. The Reformers, and indeed to some degree their predecessors, reacted strongly against many of these concepts and against the whole ethos of theology to which they belonged. There was, of course, a reaffirmation of scriptural ideas. But behind that, their approach may be described as fundamentally humanistic. This was true in two senses. First, it was literary before it was conceptual: there was an attempt to let the texts, chiefly scriptural but also patristic, give their plain meaning. Second, it was concerned with Christ the man or – more formally – Christ's humanity. Thus, for example, Erasmus' teaching on the eucharist focusses chiefly on the believer's assimilation into mind and heart of the inspiring personal example of Jesus. Though the leading Reformers used more conceptual categories, they were nevertheless deeply influenced by this tendency. Hence their concern (so literalistic, as it often seems to us) with the present location of Christ's human (though glorified) body, and their difficulty in seeing that the central eucharistic language involved a multiplicity of senses, each shading into another. Hence, too, their stress on spiritual (which we might almost translate 'imaginative' – their tendency moves theology somewhat in the direction of poetry) communion with Christ in the receiving of the sacrament. And hence

the viewing of the eucharist as a kind of passion play which revitalizes saving faith in the believer by making possible the devout recalling of Christ's death. In this last line of thought, common in Lutheran piety, we find once more something which is peripheral to the eucharist in itself: if this is what it signifies, then a sermon or a dramatic production will serve as well. The eucharist becomes an enacted preaching of the word. If not dispensable in practice (for the Lord instituted it), it is hard to see it as essential in theory.

But alongside these developments, the Reformers also worked within the terms of the existing scholastic ideas. The question of the relationship between the sacrifice of Calvary and that of the altar remained a live one. Only now, because of the more vivid sense of Scripture and of Christ's human life and death, awareness of the uniqueness and all-sufficiency of the cross was so dominant that the eucharist had to be denied its sacrificial character (in the traditional senses) altogether. In the light of the new sensitivity, traditional formulations bristled with difficulties. Two of the three propositions which we listed under 5 (p.89) – 'Christ is daily immolated mystically' and 'the eucharist is an unbloody sacrifice' – now seemed to fail to make the distinction between cross and eucharist anything like sharp enough. *Memorial*, however, remained acceptable, and was the term which most clearly linked old teaching and new. To see the eucharist as a memorial of Calvary made no inroads upon either the pastness or the uniqueness of Christ's sacrificial death. Still, there were changes, even in this area. Whereas formerly the eucharist had been 'the memorial sacrifice', now it became 'the memorial of the sacrifice'. At the verbal level, much came to turn on the delicate oscillation (first found as long ago as Tertullian) between *representation* and *re-presentation*. We may note, for example, Ridley's admission in 1555 that the eucharist 'is offered after a certain manner, and in a mystery, and as a representation of that bloody sacrifice; and he doth not lie, who saith Christ to be so offered'. To say that was to go as far as possible to meet traditionally-minded opponents (when one was on trial for one's life).

Because the whole way of conceiving the leading theological categories had become more realistic and humanistic, certain old ways of thinking were now quite excluded. Thus, for Calvin, to speak of an unbloody sacrifice was nonsense: the very notion of sacrifice involved death and blood-shedding. 'Sacrifice' meant something quite definite and vivid, so the traditional phrase was a contradiction in terms. Similarly, because Christ's glorified body is in heaven, here below all we can possibly do concerning his death is to commemorate it – and that is a very luminous and strong thing to do. Not surprisingly, Calvin can say that the (old) mass positively erases 'the true and unique death of Christ' and (here is the point) 'drives it from the memory of man'. Memory is the faculty relevant to the matter, and we remember by giving sole attention to the factual death of Calvary that happened once, long ago (*Institutes* IV.18.5). Other Reformers, like Zwingli, write in similar vein.

7. *The sacrifice of praise.* Not that the Reformers eliminated all use of sacrificial language. Quite the contrary, some old phrases now received a new lease of life. Far from trying to dam up all talk of sacrifice in relation to the eucharist, they preferred to divert it into satisfactory channels. Apart from the emphasis on the eucharist as the memorial of Christ's unique sacrifice (thus making the eucharist itself firmly a non-sacrifice), the term occurs in three other shapes. First, the sacrifice of praise and thanksgiving.

This phrase had a venerable history, notably in the canon of the Roman mass; but now it was used for a purpose to which it was admirably suited, the decontamination of the sacrificial idea. For its effect was to place the eucharist firmly on a level with all other Christian acts of prayer and worship. This purpose was quite deliberate. Thus, Bucer wrote in 1545 that when the Fathers called the eucharist 'the offering of Christ' they meant the offering of prayer and praise, and that these sacrifices 'ought to be found in all holy assemblies, even though the holy supper be not celebrated in them'. The same line is followed by the English Reformers, like Cranmer and Ridley.[4] This phraseology was intended to restore to the idea of sacrifice its proper place in relation to Christian worship. But inevitably, because of the polemical context, it could hardly appear other than negative in its bearing on eucharistic doctrine. While it at least witnessed to the 'offering', Godward character of all Christian worship, including the eucharist, it failed to give any satisfactory account of the eucharist's specific place within it.

8. *The sacrifice of selves.* The Reformers also applied sacrificial language to the worshippers' offering of themselves to God. This was a more positive doctrine, for it was specifically connected with the eucharist's distinctive and central features. But it is important to note what it affirmed and what it rejected. There was no question of the believers' offering themselves to God in the perfect offering of Christ, made present (however that might be seen) in the eucharist. Rather, by receiving the sacrament, the believers enacted

the memorial of the sacrifice of Calvary, and in the strength of that outward sign were then (and then only) able to offer themselves to God for his service. It is essentially a post-communion offering (see the first post-communion prayer in the Book of Common Prayer of 1552 and 1662). The sacrifice is the communicant's devout response to the gift bestowed upon him in the sacrament. It does not consist of the sacramental elements themselves and is not connected with the consecration of the elements.

Behind this idea lies the Protestant sense of the centrality of faith in the all-sufficiency of Christ's sacrifice, a faith renewed by the experience of the rehearsal of Christ's passion in the eucharist. Faith renewed leads directly to the renewal of self-offering.

Though its context is certainly eucharistic, it must be said that this theme, like that of the offering of praise, is not worked closely into a coherent pattern of specifically eucharistic doctrine. Self-offering is what is primarily in view; the eucharist is simply one among a number of contexts in which it may be expressed and reaffirmed.

9. *The sacrifice of alms.* In replacing old ideas of eucharistic sacrifice, the Reformers discerned not only a sacrifice of praise and a sacrifice of selves, but also a sacrifice of gifts in the shape of the alms of the people. Conceptually, this raises nothing fresh: it is simply 2 above (p.86) put into a new context.

What is more interesting about the Reformers' formulations on this subject is the way in which broadly Platonist assumptions still governed the matter. It was taken for granted that there was such a thing as 'sacrifice in the eucharist', only Catholic theologians discerned it mistakenly. The task of theology was to formulate it correctly, and the procedure, in effect, was to discover, if possible on ancient precedent, features of the true (i.e. Reformed) eucharistic theology to which sacrificial language could suitably be applied.

This same mode of thought has also been apparent at the merely verbal level, particularly in high Anglican teaching. Sometimes it seems that writers have been as it were bemused by the word 'sacrifice' itself, and have felt impelled to draw into a single pattern of thought every approved use of the word in eucharistic contexts, whether from early Christian writers, or from liturgies of past or present. The result has tended to be statements which, however stimulating they may be devotionally, defy attempts to reduce them to logical coherence.[5]

10. *The sacrifice of the church.* The Reformation insistence upon

the offering of 'ourselves, our souls and bodies' has a more Catholic counterpart in the idea of the offering of the church. Both Roman Catholic and Anglican theologians (notably R. I. Wilberforce) have contributed to its elaboration.

Whatever the resemblances, the conceptual setting is quite different from the comparable Protestant doctrine. It stems from the Pauline and Johannine teaching about life 'in Christ', and found typical formulation in relation to the eucharist in St Augustine's words: 'Since the Church is his body, she learns through him to offer herself' (*De Civitate Dei* X.20). It revived when there was a slackening (chiefly in this country) of a strict application to the eucharist of the categories of propitiation and satisfaction. Characteristically, it is expressed in terms of the body offering itself in the eucharist, in Christ the head, to the Father. In effect, it is an application to the eucharistic context of the ecclesiology of the Epistle to the Ephesians. This pattern has the merit of binding the idea of sacrifice in the eucharist to more fundamental doctrine, neglect of which is only too apparent in so many of the other patterns. It sets the eucharist, seen as a firmly Godward act, firmly in the setting of christology and ecclesiology. Its weakness is a too rigid dependence upon the particular image of the body of Christ.[6]

11. *The heavenly altar.* Seventeenth-century Anglicanism was also responsible for bringing another ancient idea into new prominence: that of the heavenly altar at which Christ's once-for-all sacrifice is eternally pleaded, while, in dependent parallelism, the church militant offers its eucharistic worship at the earthly altar (as once, provincial ceremonies mirrored those of the imperial court in Rome). This affords a pictorial framework within which a number of the other concepts may be seen; it does not conflict with other ideas but combines with them relatively easily. This of course is also the root of its weakness. Its ineradicably pictorial and analogical character makes it hard to fit into a more abstract conceptual pattern, if coherence is to be maintained.

The roots of it are so distinguished and comprehensive that it was bound to become prominent. They range from the Epistle to the Hebrews, through patristic texts and the Roman canon to the Protestant emphasis on the all-sufficiency of Calvary. It was a satisfying doctrine for those (like the seventeenth-century high Anglicans) who wished to give more positive content to the traditional, above all patristic, sacrificial teaching in relation to the eucharist, while, at least to their own satisfaction, not abandoning their Protestant heritage. Protestantism itself has remained unconvinced by a model which seems to threaten the uniqueness of Calvary.

12. *Liturgy as the biography of Christ.* Among all the ways in which the eucharist has been thought of in sacrificial terms, this is both eccentric and conceptually independent of all the rest. It is the notion of the form of the liturgy itself as a retracing of the steps of the life, death and resurrection of Christ. Used mainly as a devotional aid, it naturally depends wholly on what are from this point of view the accidents of liturgical development. Thus, the pattern works when the *Gloria in Excelsis* is at the beginning of the Mass, to represent the nativity, but not when it comes at the end. According to this view, the canon contains, after the recital of the story of the Supper, the offering of the sacrifice – the rehearsal of Calvary. This scheme serves to accentuate the realism of a quasi-identification of Calvary and eucharist, to which other patterns also lead. So it gained a certain amount of rather dubious support.

4. Sacrifice and the Eucharist

What conclusions emerge from this disentangling of threads? The analysis is in some ways discouraging. The first entry of the term 'sacrifice' into discussions of the eucharist was, from the point of view of its central meaning, tangential. Its use in the course of Christian history has often been peripheral or positively mistaken. Peripheral in the sense that it has brought out features of the eucharist that belong to the conceptually less strict sphere of piety or are anyhow incidental to the rite's main significance. Mistaken in the sense that some of the most common lines of thought on the subject fail to do justice to the christology, soteriology and ecclesiology upon which surely sound eucharistic doctrine ought to rest.

But there is another side to the matter. The very fact that sacrificial language has been so persistent in thought about the eucharist, the very fact that it has taken so many different and often original turns indicates that, however tortuous or muddled the thought has often been, 'sacrifice' is a useful and perhaps indispensable concept in this connection. There are grounds for declining to be wholly discouraged from its use. Chiefly, 'sacrifice' has one property which other images lack and which needs to be included in any account of the believer's relationship with God: totality of self-offering. It is true that the term is no longer current coin. It is also true that some uses of it have neglected this very feature which is its strength (e.g. the idea of the eucharist as a sacrifice of praise and thanksgiving).

Nevertheless, this remains its most useful feature, for how else can man come before God except in the attitude of sacrifice and with the intention to offer all? The question is, how ought this to be articulated in relation to the eucharist? How may the image be suitably exploited? And how can it be brought into relation to Christ's life and death which possess the same character and with which the eucharist is indissolubly linked? Is the search for a fully satisfactory use of this language any more hopeful now that we are better placed to look at it as language, that is, as a tool for our use, and now that we are more coolly aware of its pedigree; or is this path too overgrown for further progress to be profitable, so that the best thing is to abandon it altogether and look for other terms?

One of the difficulties with most of the commonest formulations involving sacrificial language is that they start too far up the conceptual ladder; that is, they presuppose more fundamental theological concepts which seem not to be fully clear, like a mountain whose summit is exposed while the lower levels are shrouded in mist. This is what we meant when we said earlier that these lines of thought fail to do justice to doctrine on which they rest. Consider statements like 'we offer Christ in the eucharist'; 'Christ pleads his sacrifice in the eucharist'; 'we unite our offering with Christ's oblation on Calvary'. These and others are all hard to expound satisfactorily once they are explored in the context of basic Christian belief (for example, about our relationship to Christ and the effect of his life and death).

They also fail another test. All of them unashamedly mix two levels of discourse and speak in one breath of heavenly 'events' and earthly actions. It may be a better procedure to start from the latter, and to give a clear account of the eucharist at that level, before going on to say what the rite signifies in terms of our understanding of God. The eucharist *is*, then, as an earthly action, a blessing and sharing of bread and wine by Christian believers, on the warrant of the Last Supper. What can this act fittingly say about God, in the light of our whole awareness of him? This is the question to ask.

In all this discussion there is one assumption which at this point needs to be brought to the surface: that the eucharist is to be seen as the act which sums up and expresses the whole Christian faith, the act which stands at the hub of Christian life – as it were, the tribal dance of the Christians, embodying and strengthening the world-outlook which binds them together. It is only if this view is held that the attempt to see it in the setting of the whole structure of Christian doctrine will arise and be taken seriously as a theological task. If on the contrary the eucharist is taken to be simply one item in Christian life alongside others, belief about it may well be regarded as a relatively autonomous subject. The validity of various ways of speaking of it will tend to be judged not by rigorous standards of consistency and coherence but rather by the different and perhaps more subjective standards of devotional suitability. The lack of conceptual interconnectedness between different ideas will be no bar to their value or to their claim to a place in Christian use. Those who see the eucharist simply as one among a number of God's gracious provisions for his people will tend to opt for this second view. Those who see it as much more central than that cannot avoid facing the fundamental questions which we have been asking.

If we take this more comprehensive approach, remembering our concern with sacrifice, we might have before us this statement of Augustine: 'A true sacrifice is any act that is done in order that we may cleave in holy union to God.' On this broad definition, the eucharist surely has a character which can be appropriately spoken of as sacrificial; but if this is more than incidental, it must be more integrally related to its specific features than a phrase like, for example, 'sacrifice of praise' implies. The general idea of the eucharist as a Godward act needs to be developed with reference to the character of the rite itself.

In other words, if eucharistic doctrine is to be satisfactory, it needs to take seriously two starting-points: the nature and will of God for us, and the character of the rite. As it is God's revealed nature to give himself with a completeness of which Calvary is the measure, and his will that we should give ourselves wholly to him, the eucharist, if it is to embody this faith, must make its expression possible. At two levels, the rite does precisely this. First, at the natural level, its framing in a shared meal brings to bear all the implications of common belief, aspiration and purpose. Second, at the level of what is almost tautology, the solemn blessing of the bread and wine serves to designate them for the very purpose of expressing what the rite is concerned to accomplish. From one point of view it 'works' at the level of psychology, for it 'conditions' the Christians to hold more firmly and to be more identified with the faith which they bring to it.[7] The tribal dance binds together the tribe. It is nevertheless the 'act' of God, through the accredited means, for it is, we believe, his will to accomplish this purpose in his people by this rite. The action of thanksgiving-cum-communion matches the purpose which it serves.

Finally, however rigidly and mistakenly the relationship of Christ's self-offering and the eucharist has often been expressed, the instinct which pressed towards identifying them was not fundamentally at fault. For wherever God acts in the cause of bringing men to true relationship with himself, he acts unreservedly as himself and exhibits always the same dependable characteristics; whether in the person of Jesus or in the sacrament of the eucharist or in any facet of the work of his grace. It is a pity that the road by which the term 'sacrifice' first entered the discussion and then subsequently developed was such as to render the proper use of this most striking image highly problematical. Over the centuries, the language of eucharistic sacrifice has turned into a minefield in which it has been hard to tread with safety, though many have shown a remarkable capacity for refusing to disintegrate even when they have been blown up. But through all vicissitudes of theology, the eucharist remains the outstanding means by which God's people bring to a focus their total corporate and individual self-offering to him, because of Jesus, who both showed us the way and gave us the rite by which to grow in it. God's gift 'in Christ' and our response 'in Christ' meet and fuse in the single act.

NOTES

1. The writer has been much helped by reflections offered by the Revd Canon E. M. B. Green.
2. Cf. M. F. Wiles, *The Making of Christian Doctrine*, Cambridge University Press 1967, pp.121f.
3. Cf. E. C. Ratcliff and A. H. Couratin, 'The Early Roman Canon Missae', *Journal of Ecclesiastical History* XX, 1969, pp.211ff.
4. See Francis Clark, *Eucharistic Sacrifice and the Reformation*, Darton, Longman and Todd 1960, pp.169ff.
5. See P. E. More and F. L. Cross (eds.), *Anglicanism*, SPCK 1951, pp.495f. for examples from the seventeenth century.
6. See E. L. Mascall, *Corpus Christi*, Longmans 1953.
7. See James Lambert, *Science and Sanctity*, Faith Press 1961, pp.44ff.

7

The Eucharistic Presence[1]

H. E. W. Turner

There is a certain theological inconsequence in discussing eucharistic presence apart from eucharistic sacrifice (which is the subject of another essay in this volume). Many would claim that the Last Supper was set in the context of the Jewish Passover, which had sacrificial overtones. In the patristic period the two themes are equally primitive, though the development of both themes took place at different speeds and in somewhat different directions. The problems in both cases are similar but not identical – how is the presence of Christ at the service or within the consecrated elements related to his presence in daily life, and how is the sacrificial note in the eucharist related to the basic and unrepeatable sacrifice of the cross? No uniform account of the relation between the two aspects of the doctrine has as yet emerged. The Jesuit de la Taille[2] insists that no serious approach to eucharistic sacrifice can be made apart from the doctrine of transubstantiation. Others again, while standing more or less firmly to the doctrine of the real presence, adopt greater reserve towards the sacrifice. Others again are content to accept both at the level of unexplained fact.

In general it is true that the fact of the eucharistic presence is more widely accepted by Christians than a corresponding doctrine of the sacrifice. Few Christians would be content with a doctrine of real absence. Even those who regard the eucharist primarily as a memorial meal speak of the presence of Christ 'as a host with his guests'.

The association of the presence of Christ with the eucharist raises few problems. He was the agent at the Last Supper, which was so closely associated both in word and deed with his impending death. The words of institution indicate some relation between the bread and wine and his own person. The link between the Last Supper and the eucharist is constituted by the command to repeat recorded by St Paul and contained in some MSS of St Luke. Despite the absence of an institution narrative in the Fourth Gospel the link between the presence of Christ and the eucharist is made even more explicit in the discourse in ch.6. The primitive ejaculatory cry 'Maranatha' ('Come, Lord,' or, 'Our Lord comes')[3] may have either an eschatological or a liturgical context or possibly both; it indicates both the desire for and the assurance of Christ's presence with his people. Lietzmann[4] even finds within the New Testament itself two traditions which might approximate to the two possibilities noted above, Christ present at the service and Christ present within the elements, though his conclusions have not commanded universal assent. More probably the quest for theological explanations as well as the rise and growth of fixed liturgical forms would naturally bring the issue into prominence in later centuries.

At any rate in the patristic period the underlying assumption of the literature is a devotional realism which can be variously expressed. The evidence is disparate in character (exegetical allusions, homiletical explanations and liturgical material). It is of varying degrees of theological penetration. But even when it is least theologically self-conscious it would make nonsense if the real presence of Christ at the service or within the elements was not a widely accepted devotional and liturgical fact. By the fourth century two main streams of interpretation began to emerge – metabolism which asserts some change in the elements, not uniformly expressed or precisely identified, and dualism which emphasizes a full co-presence of bread and wine and body and blood. With some notable exceptions these two streams correspond with two parallel traditions in christology, the one which stresses the primacy and centrality of God the Word in the incarnate Lord, and the other which starts from the full co-presence of divinity and humanity in his total person.

A recent Roman Catholic writer[5] calls attention to the fact that the first context in which the eucharist was understood was not metaphysics but action. This is obviously a proper framework to employ. Christ's command was 'Do this', and the eucharist was (and still is) an action to be performed rather than a doctrine to be believed. The rise and development of liturgies as well as the permanent practice of liturgizing ensured that this context could never be completely forgotten. The eucharistic presence of Christ (however else it is explained or clarified) is always a dynamic

The Eucharistic Presence

presence. The quest for theological explanations led in course of time to the virtual replacement of one framework of reference by another. In an age in which ontology was the accepted idiom both for philosophy and theology, a marked (though subtle) change comes over the doctrine of the eucharistic presence. As in the doctrine of grace there was a tendency to 'reify' or to interpret what is essentially a person or a personal and person-directed activity of the gracious God into a thing (a supernatural quiddity), resulting in what may be called a 'commodity theory' of grace, so in eucharistic theology there arose a parallel tendency to interpret the presence in ontological or entitative terms or to replace the question 'Who is present?' by the enquiry 'What is present?'. The real presence of Christ (understood dynamically) became replaced by the assertion that the body and blood of Christ were present *realiter* under the forms of bread and wine.

In both doctrines the system of explanation as it were 'slipped a cog' from that which is appropriate for persons to one which is appropriate for things. The logic of personal relations is very different from that of our relation with things, and many problems both about grace and with regard to the eucharist are due to attempts to articulate insights about our relationship with God in categories which are only suited for the expression of our relationship to things. This is a logical error as well as a source of theological misunderstanding.

The Reformation can best be understood as a wholly justified protest against theological statements and devotional attitudes to which this whole tendency in the doctrines of grace and of the eucharist inevitably led.

A more hopeful and irenic approach to the doctrine of the eucharist presence seems to lie in a return to more dynamic and personalist categories or to start from the question 'Who is present?' and to go on from there.

It may be objected that the biblical narratives themselves exclude this possibility and that the phrases 'This is my body' and 'This is my blood' require an entitative approach. It is common ground to all scholars that neither the Bible nor the Fathers had any terms which correspond exactly to the modern concept of personality; it would be sheer anachronism to expect that they should. The biblical usage of body is not contrasted with 'person'; it points towards it. In Hebrew and Aramaic there are two words which can be translated by the Greek *sōma* used in the words of institution – *gūph* (corpse) or *bāśār* or *biśrī* (flesh). If our Lord used the former at the Last Supper, it can only have a metaphorical or at least a proleptic significance (looking forward to the cross); if he used the latter, then neither the Greek *sōma* nor the Latin *corpus* is an adequate rendering. Although Hebrew has the term *nephesh*, which is translated *psuchē* in Greek, *bāśār* is never contrasted with *nephesh* in Hebrew in the same way as *sōma* with *psuchē* in Greek. St Paul seems to have the Hebrew usage in mind in such passages as Rom. 12.2; Phil. 1.20.[6]

This evidence leaves open such a paraphrase as 'This is I myself, my life enriched and made available by my death', which seems to catch the authentic echo of the institution narratives. The absence of a copulative in Aramaic does not decide the relation between the subject and the predicate either way. The absence of accents in Greek manuscripts makes it impossible to determine what emphasis should be placed on the Greek copulative in the passage.

If the words are understood in an entitative manner serious theological difficulties arise. Despite the great eucharistic hymn of St Thomas Aquinas 'gives himself with his own hand', the situation at the Last Supper where Jesus was physically present and yet points to the bread as his body is difficult to explain satisfactorily. Reference to the risen, ascended and glorified body in the church's eucharist is exposed to the problems to which the Black Rubric at the end of the 1662 rite plainly points, even after taking into account the contemporary notions of locality and corporeality which it assumes. The concept of a special eucharistic body (if anything other than this is meant) is either misleading or superfluous and calls for the exercise of Occam's razor.

It is therefore impossible, like Luther at the Marburg Colloquy with Zwingli (1529), to chalk *Hoc est corpus meum* on the table and to leave it at that. The alternatives 'is' and 'means' (*est* and *significat*) stake a claim for and register a protest against an entitative interpretation of the words of institution, as it was currently understood. A mistaken statement of the problem is also involved, since 'meaning' is included in and not contrasted with 'existence'.

The copulative 'is' is a more complicated word than appears at first sight. It can express strict identity or self-identification as in Acts 9.4 (Saul, Saul why persecutest thou me?) or Matt. 25.40 (Inasmuch as ye have done it to the least of these my brethren, ye have done it unto me). It can be used by an artist pointing to a masterpiece, an author to a book or even a founder to an institution and saying 'This is me'. In such cases there is always a note both of achievement and of sacrifice. Since the Last Supper pointed forward alike to the cross and to the church, both are found in the Last Supper, which is linked immediately to the cross and mediately to the church's eucharist in which Christ's personal self-giving at cost continues in his church 'until he come'.

If, then, the real presence of the body and blood can be interpreted as an expression of the fact that Christ himself is really and fully present as a person at the service or within the consecrated elements, some theological puzzles with regard to eucharistic theology disappear, though not at the expense of the central mystery. The whole eucharistic experience is set in a more appropriate context and 'pegged in' at a more relevant level of understanding. Some Anglicans, however, regard the statement that Christ is really and dynamically present as something less than the full meaning of the eucharist. To look for any more entitative content in the words of institution is to look for something less or something more which is difficult to specify and still more to justify.

A partial anticipation of the view expounded here has been widely current in Reformed circles which speak of Christ as 'really but spiritually present'. This represents negatively a protest against an entitative treatment of the elements but positively an attempt to move towards a personalist approach. Unfortunately, however, the word 'spiritually' without further clarification is vague and may even beg important questions. The relation between the presence and the elements is left unexplored. Some relationship must exist but, as it stands, the formula may have more to say about what it is not than to offer a convincing suggestion as to what it is.

Both the doctrine and the experience of the eucharistic presence presuppose a double polarity of the givenness of the presence and the faith of the recipient. The tragedy of the Reformation deadlock was that both sides emphasized one element in the polarity at the expense of the other, although some qualifications were made on each side with different degrees of success. The aim of the *ex opere operato* formula (that the sacraments confer grace *in virtue of the act performed*) was to express the givenness of the presence in entitative terms, while the Reformed insistence upon the *sola fide* (by faith alone) was a much needed correction of the imbalance by the reassertion of the necessity for faith. But, as more widely in the doctrine of grace, so more specifically with regard to the eucharistic presence, nothing can be taken which is not first given, but equally what is given is given in order to be taken.

Yet even at this period the two-sided nature of eucharistic experience was not completely overlooked. For all its reaffirmation of the *ex opere operato* principle Trent[7] adds two important qualifications. The eucharist was instituted 'to be consumed' (*ut consumatur*) and, more directly, the *ex opere operato* was restricted 'to those who do not place an obstacle in the way' (*obicem non ponentibus*). The phrase was too minimal to satisfy the Reformers, though the explanation of recent Roman Catholic theologians that it was deliberately pitched in a low key to cover the sacrament of infant baptism (where conscious faith could not be presupposed) is at least possible. On the Reformation side, Luther with his emphasis on the 'in, with and under' formula to express the relation of the body and blood to the bread and wine is the most outstanding example of an attempt to provide for the element of givenness. Calvin's description of the elements as 'efficacious signs' (*signa efficacia*) is a different and perhaps a less striking effort in the same direction. As Père Bouyer, a former Lutheran, notes,[8] the Reformation stood for the reassertion of a subjectivity which had been swamped or overlooked in the massive institutional and theological objectivity of the mediaeval period. His charge that this necessary subjectivity led inevitably to subjectivism may be neither as true nor as inescapable as he believes.

How can the interpretation of the eucharist in personalist terms handle this problem of its double objectivity and subjectivity? This can best be explored by discussing various descriptions associated with the givenness of the presence.

(*a*) The real presence has been classically understood as a special presence. When this was understood in entitative terms, this led to the abuse of the practice of reservation for purposes of adoration and not merely for extended communion. Phrases like 'the prisoner in the tabernacle' or the encouragement of 'little visits to Jesus' and the practice of Benediction with the reserved elements are happily not part of Anglican language or practice, at least on any significant scale. Part, however, of the evangelical objection to reservation even for extended communion is that it might encourage by oversight or intention a theology or practice of this type.

No doctrine of the eucharistic presence which marks it off too sharply from the general awareness of Christ in daily life can be regarded as satisfactory. Christ in church and Christ in chores mutually support and involve each other. Here there is a parallel between the general immanence of God in creation and his special intervention in the incarnation. Neither makes the other superfluous and the one supports and undergirds the other. Using the personalist model, there is a general awareness of two people who love each other, but this does not exclude special encounters with each other. The common factor both in the doctrine and the model is givenness. Whether the givenness in both cases differs in degree or in kind might be disputed, but, like most questions of this type, it is probably unanswerable and may even be an improper question. In human relationships we are thoroughly familiar with the notion of a graduated givenness. I hope that I give myself more richly to my wife or my pupils than I do to the milkman when I order the milk or pay the bill.

(*b*) In what sense can the real presence be described as a 'mediated' givenness? Here a distinction between mediation and manipulation is necessary. There is some evidence that the danger of confusion here is not wholly unreal. The phrase 'to make God' (*faire Dieu*) has no higher authority than the Curé d' Ars, but a fuller and more theologically reputable statement occurs in a pastoral letter of a bishop of Salzburg in 1905.[9] He writes of 'the priest's power over the body and blood of our Lord – the power to consecrate, to make present the body of our Lord with the precious blood under the forms of bread and wine. 'He has set priests in his place so that they may repeat the same sacrifice which he offered. To them he has transferred power over his sacred humanity; to them he has given the same power over his body ... he is here at the disposal of the Catholic priest.' It is only fair to note that such language would almost certainly not be used by a responsible Roman Catholic theologian of the post-Vatican II period. The passage, however, calls attention to a real danger.

The distinction which is being made here is crucial. It is characteristic of things that they can be manipulated and of persons, in so far as they are treated as persons, and not merely as tools or hands, that they cannot. Bread and wine are things which we use for our common purposes, but God would not be God if he could be 'used' by man. God giving himself to man in response to man's needs is one thing, God being 'used' by man quite another. There is a danger in mediation language, even when it is not carried to the lengths of manipulation, that it may concentrate on the gift at the expense of the giver. This is considerably lessened if the eucharist is interpreted in personalist and not in entitative terms.

For some, the dangers which we are discussing may appear so real that they may prefer to dispense with the concept of mediation altogether; others will regard then as occasional exaggerations which can be tolerated without detriment to the principle. The maxim that abuse does not destroy use may be relevant here.

On personalist premises, however, the problem is greatly eased, provided that mediation is always firmly treated as self-mediation and the maxim that Christ is the principal agent in every sacrament is fully applied. On the model of human persons mediation raises no special problems, not only because man is a psychosomatic entity (and therefore himself an embodied being), but also because he inevitably uses natural media for the expression of his personal concerns. In God's dealings with men in the church, too, it would be surprising if he could not use natural media as the instruments of his self-giving in Christ. It is an important and widely accepted principle in eucharistic theology that the presence is a sacramental presence and therefore operates under the category of a sign (*in genere signi*). Even on personalist premises there is need for a theology of the elements, though it will naturally take on a different form from that demanded by an entitative scale of treatment.

(*c*) In what sense can the eucharistic presence be described as a 'localized presence'? The very form of the question suggests a transition from personalist to entitative terms. An Oxford colleague of mine, who was both an agnostic and a scientist, once put the direct question 'Can you reserve a presence?'. I could only reply that it might be possible to reserve that with which a presence was associated and to which it was in some way linked. There is no doubt that the evangelical objection to practices like genuflexion to the consecrated elements is based upon theological suspicions on the point.

It might be objected that some measure of localization follows inevitably from the principle of mediation. With regard to the incarnation, which many regard as closely parallel theologically to the doctrine of the eucharist, we may recall Professor Mascall's statement:[10] 'There is one and only one historical individual in whom the Word was made flesh, Jesus of Nazareth, the Son of Mary, born in a particular stable in the town of Bethlehem on a particular night in a particular year.' Yet, however gladly we may assent to this succinct statement of the saving particularity of the incarnation, the localization in his humanity of the Son of God, it needs to be qualified by the doctrine that he was everywhere reigning as king in the universe even when he was living within the limits of the incarnation. This is a frequent theme in the Fathers and receives special emphasis in the christology of Calvin.[11]

The personalist model helps to put the problem of localization in better perspective. The question often assumes that God's presence is comparable to that of a material object. Persons, however, are not necessarily located in space, at least not in the same way as material objects. In particular, personal relationships can be very little subject to spatial limitations. The connection here under modern conditions is more complex than might at first sight appear. A letter, a message, a telephone call, a wireless talk or a television broadcast are all examples of personal relationships, but their connection with localization is manifold and variable. It is easy to press the question too hard even with human personalities. Localization, though often, indeed usually, related to mediation, cannot simply be identified with it. That is why the location of the presence in the rite as a whole, or in a particular moment of consecration or reception, or even merely in the faith of the recipient, is a profitless question. All these factors are involved, but the problem of localization cannot be answered without reference to them all. The givenness of the presence is not set at risk by our failure to return a simple answer to the question of location of the type which an entitative approach would require.

With faith, the other component in the polarity, we can deal more briefly, partly because much that needs to be said has already been discussed in describing the Reformation deadlock, and partly because it has never given rise to the acute problems which have historically beset the givenness of the eucharistic presence. We have seen that the *ex opere operato* formula needs to be balanced by more adequate qualifiers than Trent found it possible to provide. The alternative formula *ex opere operantis* (that sacraments confer grace by virtue of the act of the doer) will not serve our needs here, for it was originally constructed to answer a different question (the effect on sacraments of the personal unworthiness of a minister), and even here it has been rejected on conclusive grounds by all the major churches. Rather, some phrase like in *modum recipientis* (according to the manner suitable to the recipient) would serve the purpose better. This is a principle which extends throughout the whole range of God's dealings with his creatures, his activity in creation, his action in history, above all in the incarnation and in the church. As Professor Macquarrie has shown us, for God, being involves a 'letting-be'.[12] In the theology of the Christian life it recurs in the relation between grace and faith, and as applied to the sacraments it may be described as the grace-faith reciprocal. The givenness of the eucharistic presence is for reception, God's grace demands (and evokes) man's responsive faith. God is the God who acts, the God who gives, but we must approach him with openness of heart or responsive faith if his giving and acting are to mean anything to us. Words like surrender and commitment are as essential to eucharistic experience as to any other encounter with God. Again, the human personal model is relevant here, whether in the minimal condition of good faith in a legal contrast or in the full mutual trust and commitment of a happy and fulfilled married life. So understood, the *ex opere operato* and the *sola fide* necessitate each other and, if *rightly articulated*, represent not incompatibles but correlatives. On two subsidiary but related questions, neither of which is fundamental to our argument, it is neither possible nor necessary to reach agreement. The emphasis on the two elements of the polarity will fall differently for different people, and within the faith component, some will stress the corporate faith of the worshipping community, others the faith of the individual communicant. The options here depend upon the doctrine of the church, the theology of the Christian life and, more intimately, upon questions of spirituality in which no one has the right to judge another even when he cannot agree himself.

Fortunately Anglicans are not committed to any particular way of expressing the relation between the presence and the elements. The reply of Lancelot Andrewes to Cardinal Bellarmine, 'We believe no less than you that the presence is real. Concerning the mode of the presence we define nothing rashly',[13] is a wise and charitable Anglican maxim. It may, however, be useful to consider the main terms which have been used historically in the light of the personalist approach to the doctrine suggested here.

(a) *Substance*. Despite its wide use in other doctrinal contexts, the fundamental objection to the term here is precisely the use of entitative thought forms in eucharistic theology. A recent Roman Catholic exposition admits that, while its use at the time was probably necessary, it requires reinterpretation, virtually amounting to replacement, today.[14] It has the additional disadvantage of lacking cash value in much contemporary philosophy. Paradoxically St Thomas Aquinas may be saying too little rather than too much about the eucharistic presence, at least for those who believe that in the last resort he is locating the presence of our Lord in a logical abstraction. As against some tendencies in mediaeval piety his view was deliberately conservative and minimizing. But his courageous and subtle doctrine appears today to be an exploration of the doctrine under the wrong categories.[15] The Lutheran variant of consubstantiation belongs to a later and coarsened form of the substance philosophy and is logically even more difficult.[16] It may be explained either as an attempt to make the minimal change in the current formula or simply as a reaffirmation of earlier eucharistic dualism, retaining not too aptly the substance terminology.

(*b*) *Value*. William Temple used the category of value to explain the relation between the presence and the elements. Indeed, he ventured to suggest that this was really the term for which St Thomas was looking. 'If Transubstantiation means Transvaluation, the objections to it partly disappear, otherwise they are very formidable.' As Temple understood value, it had both objective and subjective implications.[17] Value does not lack objectivity since it resides in an object or a person, but equally it implies a valuing mind. This might take care of the grace-faith reciprocal, and find appropriate liturgical expression in the consecration-reception rhythm. It is, therefore, easily adapted to a personalist context. How far, however, value in this sense is a meaningful philosophical term today is questionable; it is certainly less widely current than it was fifty years ago.

(*c*) *Sign*. Here we return to the use of sign or symbol language which has been persistently and rightly used of sacraments throughout the whole history of Christian thought. In the early church, words like symbol, sign, type, figure, resemblance (*homoiōma*) were freely used in connection with the eucharist, though scholars are not agreed about the context in which they were set. Particularly in the Origenist tradition with its strong Platonic emphasis, the general drift of the teaching, together with the almost complete change to metabolist language in the fourth century, suggests the implication: 'Granted that we know that we must assert the continued existence of bread and wine, let us concentrate our attention upon the really significant fact about the eucharist, the eternal content which is vehiculated through these creatures of time and space.' In the West and to a lesser extent at Antioch, the same language was used with a rather different nuance: 'Granted that body and blood are present, let us not forget the continuing presence of bread and wine.'[18] Already, it seems, the use of sign language displays a certain ambivalence.

Through St Augustine the use of sign language continued into the mediaeval period. Thus St Thomas Aquinas maintains in a pregnant and almost untranslateable phrase *'sacramenta significando causant'* (sacramental causality operates on the plane of signification or meaning).[19] A recent commentator explains the principle as follows. Sacraments signify what they effect and effect what they signify. They have therefore two characteristics, signification (their character as signs) and efficiency (their character as causes). But the former is their definition in the strict sense, the latter a property or distinguishing feature. Although these two features are inseparably united, they must not be confused with each other.[20]

The anathema of the Council of Trent was directed not against teaching of this kind, but against the interpretation of sign language in Reformed and particularly in Zwinglian circles. For Zwingli, sacraments are bare or mere signs (*nuda signa*), whereas Calvin's description of them as 'efficacious signs' (*signa efficacia*) is alike more realistic and more adequate. One of the most impressive and encouraging features of modern Roman Catholic theology has been the rehabilitation of sign language which marks a return behind Trent to the earlier sources, and its use with good effect both with regard to the presence and the sacrifice in the doctrine of the eucharist.[21] The most recent interpretation here is that transignification or a change of meaning or significance might be an acceptable contemporary gloss on transubstantiation in the light of the many objections to which it is exposed. This approximates rather closely to Temple's suggestion of transvaluation which has been discussed earlier in this essay. This is a hopeful and constructive suggestion which has much to commend it.

In view of two other essays in this collection by Mr Lucas and the Bishop of Kingston it is unnecessary here to offer an extended treatment of the category of sign or symbol. But some explanation of its ambivalence both in the early church and at and since the Reformation period ought at least to be attempted. It is certainly curious that the same term could be used both by St Thomas Aquinas and Zwingli with entirely different results.

What is known as the picture or resemblance theory of symbols, a supposed natural congruity or aptitude on the part of the sign to represent the thing signified, is probably historically part of the story. This is expressed succinctly by Tillich as follows, although it will be seen that his distinction between sign and symbol is not adopted here: 'The sacramental material is not a sign pointing to something foreign to itself. To put it in terms of the theory of symbolism, the sacramental material is not a sign but a symbol. As symbols the sacramental materials are intrinsically related to what they express.'[22] The distinction between 'foreign' and 'intrinsic' may be important, but the hint of the portrait or resemblance theory of signs must be treated with great reserve.

There are, however, difficulties here. Historically it is doubtful whether the theory is by itself a sufficient explanation of our problem. As a candidate for truth in its own right it fails almost completely to account for the most important and influential class of signs that we know and use, language itself. Words are signs, but there is rarely any resemblance whatever between the sound or shape of a word and what it means. Its significance lies not in any degree of resemblance but in its use in a consistent way according to certain linguistic conventions which constitute the language or culture within which the word is understood.

More important for the understanding of our problem is the use of two different contexts at the Reformation period to resolve the ambivalence of the word 'sign'. These may be described respectively as the contexts of continuity and discontinuity between the sign and the thing signified. Care must be taken not to identify the distinction suggested here with resemblance and lack of resemblance. The Reformers, especially Zwingli, in their use of sign language reasoned as follows: 'a sign, and therefore discontinuous with the thing signified'. Thus for Zwingli the sacraments as signs are substitutes for what is absent. The difficulty here is twofold. It denies any causality or efficiency to sacraments, and travesties what even under human conditions it means to be a sign. Thus a flag not only represents but evokes patriotism. A kiss stimulates as well as expresses love. A 'nudum' banknote would be a most ineligible form of currency. The doctrine of Calvin is at least not exposed to the first objection.

The context in which the term 'sign' is set in mediaeval and more recent Catholic theology is completely different. A sign is an indication of something which is present, but not in its natural mode or in the way in which we should expect to find it. The context here is rather 'a sign, and therefore continuous with what is signified'. Transignification is therefore no mere capitulation to the Reformed emphasis, since the antithesis between meaning and existence is completely overcome by the context in which it is employed. Meaning is part of existence and must not be set in opposition to it. The Reformation distinction between *est* (is) and *significat* (means) in the exegesis of the words of institution raised a real problem at the risk of mistaking the point at issue. The Reformed suspicion of the translation 'is' was a justified protest against an entitative interpretation, but led to a questionable divorce between meaning and existence. The modern Roman Catholic recovery of sign language reunites meaning and existence, and rightly modifies (at least by implication) the entitative assumptions to which the Reformers took strong and justifiable exception.

A personalist model taken from our reaction to the receipt of a greetings telegram on a festive occasion may help to clarify this suggestion of the two contexts in which sign language can be understood. We may say 'Well, he might have made the effort to come himself', when there is reason to believe that its despatch is an effort to save trouble or inconvenience, or it may be taken as in effect a personal appearance, though not in the way which the sender might wish or the recipient desire. The dichotomy between meaning and existence is more readily resolved on personalist than on entitative premises.

The aim of this essay has been tentative and exploratory, to set the doctrine of the eucharistic presence in a personalist and not an entitative framework, rather than to expound a particular, still less a new theory of the eucharistic presence. The Anglican approach as set out in the quotation from Lancelot Andrewes still represents our stance in the matter. The defence of a legitimate theological pluralism expounded by Professor Wiles elsewhere in this volume merits careful consideration. At some stages in the argument of this essay due care has been taken not to foreclose issues which the personalist framework seems to leave open. The theological position of the author is already familiar to some of his readers, and the general drift of the argument as well as occasional indications of personal preferences will probably reinforce this impression. But it is no part of the function of a Doctrine Commission or of a series of essays arising out of its deliberations to act as a sounding board for particular traditions within the church, but rather to theologize together and to see how we get on and what emerges.

Within this personalist framework, it is possible to assert a real, personal presence in action at or in the eucharist (in the senses noted above). This is the 'given' alike in doctrine and in experience, but it must be balanced by the element of responsive faith, both corporate and individual. Only so, it seems, can the objective and the subjective, the given and the taking of the given be seen in proper perspective.

The special nature of the presence, whether in degree or in kind, can be successfully maintained on these premises, provided that it is held firmly together with the more general awareness of Christ in daily life. The principle of mediation, the dynamic presence of Christ using material media can also be defended with somewhat more stringent safeguards. The localization of the presence and the meaning that can be assigned to the phrase must be left an open question.

The precise relation between the presence and the associated elements is not a matter on which dogmatism is possible. None of the categories proposed are free from difficulty. The traditional language of sign seems less exposed to problems than any other, provided that the false dichotomy between meaning and existence can be satisfactorily avoided. Perhaps the view that by consecration the elements become charged with a new and additional meaning as the media or vehicles of Christ's presence given in action, and that this meaning becomes henceforth part of their existence for the purposes for which the eucharist was instituted, is less exposed to difficulty than any other. The eucharist remains on any showing the sacrament of encounter with Christ, the action through which God's people are fed with the bread of life, which is also the bread of heaven.

NOTES

1. The author gratefully acknowledges his debt to Mr J. R. Lucas, a fellow member of the Doctrine Commission and author of another essay in this book, for many valuable suggestions. The author's opinions, and above all his errors, remain his own.
2. M. de la Taille, *The Mystery of Faith*, Sheed and Ward 1930.
3. I Cor. 16.22; *Didache* 10 (in Aramaic); cf. Rev. 22.20 (in Greek).
4. H. Lietzmann, *Mass and Lord's Supper*, E. J. Brill, Leiden 1953.
5. J. Betz, *Die Eucharistie in der Zeit der griechischen Väter*, Vol.I, Freiburg, 1961, pp.xxiii-xxvii (this study is unfortunately as yet unfinished).
6. K. Grobel, '*Soma* as Self or Person in the Septuagint', *ZNTW* 21, 1954, pp.252-9.
7. E. Schillebeeckx, *The Eucharist*, Sheed and Ward 1968, pp.23-86. This section, on the definition of the Council of Trent (1545–63), is particularly important.
8. L. Bouyer, *Du Protestantisme à l'église*, Paris 1955.
9. Pastoral Letter of the Bishop of Salzburg, 1905.
10. E. L. Mascall, *Christ, the Christian and the Church*, Longmans 1946, p.19.
11. This is the doctrine of the so-called *extra Calvinisticum* – the existence of the Son of God not only in the flesh but also (*etiam*) outside it (*extra carnem*). In its developed form it represented a protest against Swabian

Lutheranism which carried the principle of the *communicatio idiomatum* to the lengths of a virtual kenosis. While the doctrine is found in Calvin, the term itself cannot be traced earlier than 1621. Among the Fathers it occurs in Athanasius, *de Incarnatione* 17; Cyril, *Ep. xvii ad Nest.* III; *Hom. Pasch.* 17; Theodore of Mopsuestia, *de Incarnatione* VII fr.; Augustine, *Ep.* lxxxvii *ad Volus*; *de Civitate Dei* IX.15.2; *de Pecc. Mer. et Remiss.* I.60 (31); and in other Fathers. It is also found in representative scholastics like Peter Lombard and St Thomas Aquinas. In the light of such evidence, E. D. Willis, *Calvin's Catholic Christology*, Luzac 1967, claims that it can as easily be called the *extra Catholicum* as the *extra Calvinisticum*.

12. J. Macquarrie, *Principles of Christian Theology*, SCM Press 1966, p.103.

13. Lancelot Andrewes, *Responsio ad Apologiam Cardinalis Bellarmini*, cited as part of extract 200 in F. L. Cross and P. E. More, *Anglicanism*, SPCK 1951, p.464.

14. J. M. Powers, *Eucharistic Theology*, Burns and Oates 1968. See the comments by E. Schillebeeckx, op.cit., pp.99-113.

15. The doctrine of transubstantiation depends upon the Aristotelian distinction between substance and accidents, the inner reality of a thing and the accidents and attributes which inhere in it or describe it. Substance attempts to answer the question 'Is there anything there?', the accidents answer the question 'What sort of a thing is there?'. As applied to the eucharist, transubstantiation means that, while the accidents of bread and wine remain unimpaired, the substance of bread and wine is changed by consecration into the substance of body and blood.

16. The doctrine of consubstantiation holds that, after the consecration of the elements, the substances of body and blood and of bread and wine co-exist in union with each other. The model of red-hot iron in which iron and fire are united with each other but remain unchanged must be regarded as suspect. It had been used much earlier in christological debate, but was rejected because of its Monophysite implications. In neither doctrinal context does it greatly assist the argument.

17. William Temple, *Christus Veritas*, Macmillan 1924, p.247.

18. Compare the discussion in F. Loofs, 'Abendmahl I', in Hauck-Herzog, *Realencyklopaedie für protestantische Theologie und Kirche* I, pp.32-8, with the parallel discussions of the evidence in A. Harnack, *History of Dogma*, Vol. IV, London 1898, ch.4, pp.281ff. Loofs consistently contrasts symbol and sign with presence; Harnack interprets the evidence in a less restricted and negative way. Harnack is generally held to have the better of the argument. My suggestions here do not correspond exactly to either, but are closer to Harnack than to Loofs.

19. St Thomas Aquinas, *de Veritate*, qu.27, art.4.

20. J. F. Gallagher, *Significando Causant. A Study in Sacramental Causality*, University Press, Fribourg 1965, traces the numerous and considerable elaborations of this theme in mediaeval and modern times.

21. For eucharistic presence see E. Schillebeeckx, op.cit., pp.100ff.,137-48; J. M. Powers, op.cit., passim; for eucharistic sacrifice see A. Vonier, *A Key to the Doctrine of the Eucharist*, Burns, Oates 1925; E. Masure, *The Christian Sacrifice*, Burns, Oates and Washbourne 1944.

22. Paul Tillich, *Systematic Theology*, Vol.III, Nisbet 1964, p.130.

8

Eucharistic Theology – The Value of Diversity

M. F. Wiles

The so-called sacrament of unity has been a notorious cause of Christian division. Is the eucharist a sacrifice? In what sense is Christ specially present in it? Issues of this kind have divided Christians bitterly from one another. Other papers in this collection consider how such issues may be approached today in a more eirenical spirit. The aim of this paper is to ask in more general terms whether a wide diversity in eucharistic understanding and practice is not only an acceptable aim but also a highly appropriate one. Just as there is widespread agreement today that no one approach to theology can claim absolute priority over all others, so we ought to expect and even to welcome the same sort of variety in eucharistic thought and piety.

Such an enquiry does well to begin at the beginning: Why do we have sacraments at all? In particular, why this one? The appropriateness of a ritual action of this kind at the heart of religious practice appears less obvious to many people today than has often been the case in the past. Yet it is not difficult to point to a widespread urge amongst human beings to join together in patterned corporate activity. Such forms of activity are not characteristic only of a primitive stage of social development. In very differing ways they are a feature of all societies at every stage of development. Sacramental activity as a whole has a grounding in the nature of man as created by God.

The basic constituents of such corporate activity are various – processions, dancing, sharing a common meal and so on. What is the significance of the church's concentration upon one particular form of sacramental activity as central to her corporate life? Here the historical link with Jesus and the early church is decisive. Even for those who are led by critical examination of the evidence to question the propriety of speaking of the eucharist as specifically instituted by Jesus, this historical link remains a clear and central factor. But even if this is what is decisive, might not the eucharist still be able to draw more widely than it does upon the varied forms of corporate activity which are natural to human societies? If, for example, the eucharist is intended to provide an expression and experience of joy and fellowship, it might seem that in our contemporary culture dancing and relaxed conversation over a drink are the most natural ways in which to make that provision. Within the liturgy there are admittedly words and actions intended to fulfil this role, but their conventional form often prevents the effective communication of these realities to us. The evaluation of a contemporary eucharistic rite ought not to be made in terms of how far it incorporates strands to be found in earlier rites but rather how far it gives expression to the underlying intentions and objectives of the eucharist. The church could not of course simply replace the eucharist with dancing and relaxed conversation, however effective they might prove in fostering joy and fellowship; for the joy and fellowship which the church seeks to promote is not just any joy and fellowship but one which derives from a response to God as made known in Jesus. The central act with the bread and wine in association with Jesus is irreplaceable if the sacramental activity is to retain its distinctively Christian meaning, but there may well be scope for its linking with a broader complex of other forms of sacramental action.

It is with this distinctive meaning of the eucharist that we must begin. In very general terms it is to be seen as expressing the given nature of the gospel; it shows that the heart of faith is a response and a receiving. This basic insight can be developed in two related but distinguishable ways.

Most obvious is its givenness as a historical phenomenon. Sacramental meals in general may have a basis in common human needs; the eucharistic sacrament derives from one particular form of such meals within the life of Judaism. Moreover, it imposes upon that particular form of sacramental meal a very specific reference to Jesus and to his death and resurrection. It is for this reason that the church has always insisted on the complementary nature of word and sacrament. In terms of practice this has been interpreted with differing degrees of rigour. It has been taken to imply that there should always be a sermon at every celebration of the eucharist; that there should always be a reading from scripture or from the gospel; that the words of institution should always be spoken. In whatever form it is implemented, the essential point is the same. The symbolism of bread and wine is capable of a wide variety of interpretation. A signification in terms of the death of Jesus is not clearly implicit in the symbols themselves. Unless accompanied (at least as a matter of normal practice) by some spoken expression of that signification, it could very easily take on quite other, even contradictory, significance. Thus it seems to be word and sacrament together that are needed to express the historical givenness of the gospel. But it still remains a very open question: how much is given with this historical character of the sacrament? The present hermeneutical debate about how to interpret the words of the gospel today is directly relevant here. It is widely agreed that the words of the gospel do not convey a clear, unchanging meaning which can be directly apprehended by us today; they have to be reinterpreted in the light of our present knowledge about the world and contemporary ways of experiencing it. So the word which accompanies the sacramental action and helps to give it its specifically Christian meaning does not give it an absolutely clear and precise meaning. It, too, requires continual reinterpretation in the same way as does the gospel text as a whole. Thus the extent of what is given in the historical character of the sacrament must not be overstated, though it certainly points to a gift of God mediated to us through the person of Jesus.

But the eucharist may also be seen as pointing in a more general way to the priority of divine grace in the experience of faith. It is possible – and indeed perfectly proper – to speak of our attempt to lay hold of that reality beyond ourselves which we call God. But faith has never been content with this perspective. Part perhaps of the intention of strong forms of a doctrine of the real presence of Christ in the sacrament has been the desire to stress that God is there, making himself present to us prior to all our attempts to lay hold of him. For many people today such a belief does not come easily – especially not in any of its more traditional forms. When the present time is spoken of as a 'non-religious' age, the intention of such language is to stress how difficult it is for very many today to acknowledge the presence or activity of a transcendent God. Moreover, in the light of an increasingly sympathetic understanding of other religions, we tend to be particularly suspicious of accounts of that presence or activity of God which limit him too narrowly to the realm of Christendom, and within specifically Christian thought suspicious of accounts which are too closely tied to particular moments within the experience of the Christian community. Yet in spite of all our difficulty in acknowledging a transcendent personal reality beyond ourselves, in spite of all of our dissatisfaction with past ways of expressing God's special activity towards us, we still wish to give expression to our sense of responding to God's initiative, of finding him present before we seek him. And here the symbolism of the eucharist is of great value. At its climax something is given to us. Our rôle is to receive. The symbolism does not necessarily imply an inroad from beyond ourselves within the rite. It can be understood without the transcendent dimension; it can be seen and experienced simply in terms of a mutual sharing at the human level. But it does lend itself to effective expression of God's prior self-giving to us. At a time when many people find such ideas religiously central but intellectually difficult to express, their embodiment in ritual action is something of especial importance.

Here, then, are two ways in which the symbolism of the eucharist can be seen to point to the givenness of the gospel. But I say 'can be seen'. The symbolism does not express such notions unambiguously or unmistakably. Symbolism never functions in that precise kind of way. The significance has to be apprehended within the symbolic action and drawn out from it. This means that there is no escape from the task of interpretation. Whenever we perform the rite, we have to do it in one particular way; this means that there are also other ways in which we do not do it. Every performance of the rite is an interpretation, whether we are consciously aware of it as such or not. And at this point we may well become aware of differing interpretations, both of which we want to affirm, but which are to some extent in conflict with one another. It may prove impossible in practice to do justice to both at the same time, however much we wish to do so. Two examples may serve to illustrate the point.

Christians affirm both the transcendence and immanence of God, his majesty and his nearness to us. We believe in a God who is wholly other than ourselves, beyond all conceiving, whose very existing is of a different mode or order from our own, but a God who is also closer to us than breathing itself, who has come to us in the person of Christ, who is known to us as and in our neighbour. Critics of Christianity have often objected that such conflicting conceptions introduce a logical incoherence into the Christian idea of God. While not succumbing to those objections we ought not to underestimate their force. It is certainly open to question whether we can give full expression to both poles of that belief in a single pattern of thought or in a single act of worship. A solemn mass at the high altar of a great cathedral may give expression to one; the small group gathered around the table in a house church to the other. The matter is not, of course, as simple as that contrast might suggest. It is possible for the two to be grasped together in some degree – not just as a compromise but as an experience transcending any intellectual synthesis of the two. An awareness of what has been called 'the transcendent in our midst' is not an impossibility. But the point remains that any way of celebrating the eucharist is bound to put its weight more one way than the other. This is at least one element in the difference of feeling that many people have experienced, between the 1662 service and Series II – and those two rites are hardly at opposite ends of the scale when one considers the full range of differing forms of eucharistic liturgy.

A second example presents the problem in a more direct and striking form. The material elements of bread and wine give forceful expression to historical continuity; they portray an identification with the action of Jesus at the Last Supper. This aspect has been so strongly felt at times by some that people have insisted not only on bread and wine, but on *unleavened* bread and *fermented* wine. But from a very early stage the elements have also been interpreted as expressive of the incarnational principle; they have been interpreted as an offering of the first fruits of man's labour, as revealing the way in which God uses and transforms the most ordinary and everyday things of our life. But they cannot symbolize this second concept in a time or place where bread or wine is not a staple commodity of the people. So the question is raised from time to time whether it might not be more appropriate in certain circumstances to use within the eucharist sandwiches and beer or rice and saké. In practice the church has remained absolutely firm on this issue. This is no doubt due primarily to the great importance which it attaches to the historical link. It may also derive from the fact that any change at this point would tend to destroy the historical symbolism almost entirely, whereas the incarnational symbolism can always be sustained in some measure – even if not in full measure – with the use of bread and wine. Nevertheless, it is clear that we have here another case of competing symbolisms. In making our choice for one aspect, we may find ourselves reluctantly but inescapably weakening some other.

The approach to the eucharist being suggested here may be illustrated by an analogy with the multiplicity of meanings to be found in Beethoven's string quartets. Their central importance for music is generally agreed. Yet it is hard to formulate what they mean in words, precisely because they are already formulated in music. So the eucharist should be expected to have a wide range of interpretation. This does not mean that there cannot be false interpretations. The wide range of admissible interpretations of the string quartets does not mean that there are not ways of taking them which are quite wrong. So there may be ways of interpreting the eucharist which must be excluded as wrong – ways, for example, which omit the transcendent dimension or the redemptive element altogether. But it does mean that no one interpretation can be claimed as the true interpretation, thereby excluding all others which cannot be fully harmonized with it.

This conviction may serve to throw light on the puzzling question whether some particular occasion is or is not a eucharist. It suggests that the form of the question is a misleading one if it is being asked with the intention of drawing a hard and fast line between what is and what is not a eucharist. It may still be of value if its intention is to help us clarify what are important features of eucharistic worship which we should expect to find there as a norm – but none of which need necessarily be required as essential for ensuring that it is a eucharist with which we have to do. Two examples from contemporary discussion may illustrate the point.

Can there be eucharists without an ordained minister as celebrant? The issue arises not only between episcopal and non-episcopal churches. Might there not be occasions when a group of Christians, not happening to include an ordained minister among their number, were engaged upon some common enterprise in the course of which it seemed highly appropriate for them (with no schismatic intention) to break bread together? Rather than consider whether such an occasion was or was not a eucharist, it might be better to indicate the ways in which it fulfilled some important aspects of eucharistic symbolism but not others. The presidency of an ordained minister at the eucharist is important because it gives expression (like the unchanging character of the elements) to the historical givenness of the sacrament; moreover, by virtue of his authorized and representative status the ordained minister is a reminder of the relationship of any particular grouping of Christians to the whole body of the church. But it is not self-evidently the case that an occasion which lacks this particular element in the total complex of eucharistic symbolism but contains perhaps many other features is *ipso facto* not a eucharist. It may deviate from the norm without necessarily ceasing thereby to be a eucharist.

A slightly different form of the same problem arises in the ecumenical context in the common worship of Christians of different confessions. Questions have been asked about the sort of distinction which we ought to make between occasions when a breaking of bread is a eucharist and occasions when it is an *agape*. The most obvious difference between the two is that between the ritual eating and drinking characteristic of the former and the sharing of the full meal in the case of the latter. It is customary to lay great stress on the importance of maintaining a very firm distinction of kind between them. But both can trace their ancestry to early eucharistic practice and both can be shown to have positive, though differing, sacramental value. May there not be a case for laying an equal stress on the possibility of both having a valuable place within the totality of a varied eucharistic practice?

What is being suggested here is in line with what has already to some degree happened in relation to the doctrine of the church. It used to seem self-evident (perhaps indeed to some it still does) that in the face of ecclesiastical division the appropriate question to ask is: Which body (or bodies) is (or are) the church and which are not? The Roman Catholic church allowed the claim only for herself; Anglicans tended to a theory which included the Roman Catholics, Orthodox and Anglican Communions, but no other – and so on. But in course of time so much was granted in terms of God's grace operating in other Christian bodies outside the true church, that the distinction between what was and what was not the church became little more than an arbitrary semantic decision. Sometimes an attempt has been made to maintain the distinction in a somewhat less rigid way by differentiating between the church and other ecclesial bodies. So in this case also the sharpness of the distinction might be softened by speaking of the eucharist over against other eucharistic activities. But that kind of distinction does not seem to offer a satisfactory resting place. It seems rather to be a kind of transitional stage on the way to a wholly different way of understanding the problem of division. Thus in relation to the church there are many today who would prefer to speak in terms of the degree to which differing Christian bodies do or do not express in their life and structure the marks to be looked for in the church as a norm. Those marks, combining as they do such contrasting elements as order and freedom, catholicity and indigenous expression, are not easily to be found harmoniously expressed in any single body. In a similar way we need perhaps to become less concerned with drawing boundaries of what is or is not a genuine eucharist and more ready to ask in what varied ways we can today give expression to that rich range of religious reality which is offered to us in the whole eucharistic tradition.

No attempt in this short paper has been made to undertake that task. Its purpose is simply to suggest a more flexible way of approaching eucharistic theology, which might help us to grasp the meaning of the eucharist not only in a more eirenical way, but at the same time with greater fullness and depth.